# SADISTIC STATISTICS

## an introduction to statistics for the social & behavioral sciences

### Second Edition

Gideon Horowitz
Adelphi University

 AVERY PUBLISHING GROUP INC.

Wayne, New Jersey

Art Director: Prof. Richard C. Karwoski
Front cover designer: Elena Zaharakos

# CONTENTS

Appendixes

(A) Tables

To Ida
and our children Debbie,
Beth, Paul, and Ned.

# ACKNOWLEDGEMENTS

This book and its author owe a great deal to numerous individuals. Foremost among these is Professor Bernice Polemis, formerly at the University of Chicago, who taught me much more about statistics than I know. Credit should also be extended to some of the authors of statistics texts, which helped me in formulating this current epic. Among them are: James L. Bruning and B.L. Kintz, authors of *Computational Handbook of Statistics* (Glenview: Scott, Foresman and Co., 1968); Wilfrid J. Dixon and Frank J. Massey, Jr., *Introduction to Statistical Analysis* (New York: McGraw-Hill, 1957); Paul A. Games and George R. Klare, *Elementary Statistics* (New York: McGraw-Hill, 1967); William L. Hays, *Statistics for Psychologists* (New York: Holt, Rinehart and Winston, 1963); and Sidney Siegel, *Non-Parametric Statistics* (New York: McGraw-Hill, 1956). I also wish to express my appreciation to the students of statistics who suffered through some of the earlier versions of this text, and whose criticisms and suggestions were invaluable.

Gideon Horowitz

# CHAPTER 1
# INTRODUCTION

Actually, this is not an introduction. It is much more of a preface. However, after years of experience, we have come to the conclusion that people never read the preface to anything, and since we do wish to bring some things to your attention, we thought it might help if we called this an Introduction.

The main purpose of this book is to present material which will help you learn the basic statistics for social and behavioral sciences. All readers come to us with a variety of anxieties. In most cases, these anxieties reach their highest level when they hear that nasty word "statistics." And in some ways, this is understandable. Many of you may have had some courses in the "hard sciences" (physics, chemistry, etc.), and at that point may have decided that you really don't want to work in these kinds of areas; others were badly traumatized by elementary school courses in mathematics, geometry or algebra, to the extent that the mere mention of a number results in severe sweating. And now you have decided to study sociology, or psychology, or social work; you are eager to work with people, to change the system, to agitate for reforms, and what are you faced with? — statistics! So, the anxiety is understandable, and undoubtedly real, and it might help if we established a few things right at the outset. In this book, we try to keep the mathematics at a rather primitive level. You will not have to know advanced algebra, trigonometry, or calculus. Furthermore, you will not have to memorize formulas. Any formula that you do need either now or later in life is available in books and can be looked up very easily. What cannot be looked up so easily, and what we hope you will learn, is when to use what kind of formula, and what kinds of statistical manipulations are appropriate for a specific purpose. In many ways, what we shall try to teach you will not really be "new." We will try to take many of the ideas and concepts with which you are already familiar and with which you deal in everyday life, and perhaps give them a slightly different meaning, or organize them more coherently, or provide you with more concrete ways of expressing them. In some ways, statistics can be viewed as a foreign language; it is not so much a matter of gaining totally new knowledge, as it is a question of learning to translate vocabulary and concepts from one language into another.

As to the underlying basic question, namely, why are statistics necessary for the social and behavioral sciences in the first place, the answer is rather simple and rather obvious, once you can step away from your anxiety somewhat and look at life more objectively. In reality, our knowledge is extremely limited, unless we are able to test what we think we know in a scientific manner. For example, there are numerous individuals who are very ready to tell you what the Black community needs or what the Hispanic community needs. Very often, as you very well know, these individuals contradict each other. As long as we speak off the tops of our heads, or according to our individualized view of the world, or according to anecdotal evidence, we really cannot get anywhere. Social workers especially are very fond of the anecdotal approach, and we have all heard stories about "the mother of 14 children who. . . ." This kind of "evidence," based upon case histories, is used and abused not only by professionals, but also by some legislators and governors; and then we object vehemently when this evidence is used to cut benefits to the elderly, for example. But it is not until we ourselves are willing to collect data through rigorous research techniques—not until we ourselves are able to produce concrete evidence—that we shall ever be able to convince law makers, administrators, and even our own colleagues that our way is better or more productive than some other approach. So that is why statistics are important. They are the tools by which we can organize, summarize, analyze, and understand our data; they thus help us attain our goals.

As to this book, you are entitled to know several things about it. Essentially, the idea for it grew out of the dissatisfaction that some of us have felt regarding current statistics books. This attempt at a different approach uses several techniques which we hope will be helpful:

1.  No knowledge on your part is taken for granted. We always start from scratch and try to explain things in the simplest way possible, realizing that this method leads, at times, to the kinds of over-simplifications which may horrify "real" statisticians.

2.  For each chapter, we provide a number of "practice sheets" which present questions and problems that enable you to deal with the material in the chapter in a more concrete fashion.

    Please note that it is of vital importance that you do the work on the practice sheets.

3.  We do make the assumption that readers using this book have had, are having, or will have additional exposure to research methodology. Consequently, some of the material presented here (on sampling or variables, for example) is extremely sketchy.

4.  In an attempt to keep you awake, and perhaps even interested, we have included some attempts at humor — at times it's corny, at times forced, but frequently hilarious (in our opinion, of course). Although no harm is intended, we wish to take this opportunity to apologize in advance to any of you who might feel offended by some of the humor.

## ORGANIZATION OF THE BOOK

In keeping with our promise to start from the very beginning, the next chapter is devoted to a review of simple things. We will then go on to discuss some basic concepts, how data should be organized, and how data should be analyzed. We will give you a minor dose of probability theory, some notions of decision-making theory, and a few tests of significance. If that sounds frightening to you at this point in time, fear not! It shall all be done in gentle stages, and you will be amazed to find that you, too, can understand what Chi square means.

# CHAPTER 2
# A REVIEW OF SIMPLE THINGS

The purpose of this chapter is to take some of the basic mathematical material which you learned way, way back and refresh your memory about it. We will also try to introduce some very simple short-cuts, which may save you time and effort for the rest of your life.

## FRACTIONS
As you undoubtedly remember, fractions are a way of dealing with parts of a thing. We will not start drawing pictures of pies at this point, but you may want to think of fractions as having two parts. The bottom part, called the denominator, tells you how many equal parts a thing has been divided into. The top part, or the numerator, tells you how many such parts you have. Thus, for example, in terms of money, if you have three quarters (75c) this could be written as it is pronounced —3/4— and what this means is that a dollar has been divided into four parts (quarters) and you have three such parts. It is sometimes very helpful, when dealing with fractions, to translate things in this way into money, or pies, or anything else of which you are especially fond.

### Addition and Subtraction
When you add or subtract two or more fractions, they must have the same denominator. In finding this "common" denominator, it is good to proceed on the basis of the humanistic principle of equity: whatever you do to the denominator you also have to do to the numerator. Let's look at a few examples:

$$\frac{1}{2} + \frac{1}{3} = ?$$

The common denominator is 6 (both 2 and 3 can be divided into 6). Then,

$$\frac{1}{2} = \frac{3}{6} \text{ and } \frac{1}{3} = \frac{2}{6}, \text{ so:}$$

$$\frac{1}{2} + \frac{1}{3} = \frac{3}{6} + \frac{2}{6} = \frac{5}{6}$$

The same procedure is used with subtraction:

$$\frac{3}{8} - \frac{3}{16} = ?$$

$$\frac{6}{16} - \frac{3}{16} = \frac{3}{16}$$

3

When you have a mixed number (a whole number plus a fraction), you have several options available:

A.  You can change everything into fractions first. This option is most useful when you have relatively small numbers. For example:

$$2\frac{3}{4} + \frac{1}{2} = \text{?}$$

$$\frac{11}{4} + \frac{1}{2} = \text{?}$$

$$\frac{11}{4} + \frac{2}{4} = \frac{13}{4} = 3\frac{1}{4}$$

B.  You can deal with the whole numbers and the fractions separately, remembering, however, to put it all together at the end. This option is easiest to use when you have larger numbers, and you want to keep the calculation in the form of fractions. For example:

$$41\frac{1}{2} + 17\frac{5}{8} = \text{?}$$

The whole numbers:   $41 + 17 = 58$

The fractions:   $\frac{1}{2} + \frac{5}{8} = \frac{4}{8} + \frac{5}{8} = \frac{9}{8} = 1\frac{1}{8}$

Put it together:   $58 + 1\frac{1}{8} = 59\frac{1}{8}$

Sometimes, in the subtraction of two mixed numbers, you may have to "borrow":

$$
\begin{array}{ccccc}
18\frac{1}{2} & & 18\frac{2}{4} & & 17\frac{6}{4} \\
-\ 3\frac{3}{4} & = & -\ 3\frac{3}{4} & = & -\ 3\frac{3}{4} \\
\hline
\text{?} & & \text{?} & & 14\frac{3}{4}
\end{array}
$$

C.  Your third option is to convert the fractions to decimals. We will deal with conversions later in this chapter.

## Multiplication

This one's easy. All you have to do is multiply all the numerators by each other, and that is the new numerator; then multiply all the denominators by each other, and you are finished. For example:

$$\frac{2}{3} \times \frac{3}{4} = \frac{6}{12} = \frac{1}{2}$$

When fractions get bigger or when several fractions are involved, a considerable amount of time can be saved if you "cancel out" (divide numerators and denominators by the same number). Let's look at two examples of the same multiplication, one done the long way and the other the short way:

$$\frac{3}{4} \times \frac{2}{3} \times \frac{4}{6} \times \frac{4}{5} = \frac{96}{360} = \frac{4}{15}$$

$$\frac{\overset{1}{\cancel{3}}}{\underset{1}{\cancel{4}}} \times \frac{\overset{1}{\cancel{2}}}{\underset{1}{\cancel{3}}} \times \frac{\overset{1}{\cancel{4}}}{\underset{3}{\cancel{6}}} \times \frac{4}{5} = \frac{4}{15}$$

What we did here was to cancel the three in the first numerator with the three in the second denominator, the four in the first denominator with the four in the third numerator, and the two in the second numerator with the six in the third denominator, leaving a three. We then multiplied: 1 x 1 x 1 x 4 for the numerator, and 1 x 1 x 3 x 5 for the denominator. Note that our answer, of course, remains the same; but we are able to deal with much smaller numbers in this way.

Here, too, mixed numbers can be changed to fractions first. For example:

$$1\frac{1}{2} \times 1\frac{1}{4} \times \frac{7}{8} = \frac{3}{2} \times \frac{5}{4} \times \frac{7}{8} = \frac{105}{64} = 1\frac{41}{64}$$

### Division
We do not divide fractions directly. In order to divide one fraction by another, we invert the second fraction and then multiply. For example:

$$\frac{3}{4} \div \frac{2}{3} = ?$$

$$\frac{3}{4} \times \frac{3}{2} = \frac{9}{8} = 1\frac{1}{8}$$

## DECIMALS
Decimals represent another way of dealing with parts of whole numbers. Thus, for example, .35 means that we have 35/100 of something; $6.47 means that we have 6 dollars and 47/100 of a dollar, or 47c.

### Addition and Subtraction
As long as you make sure you have the decimal points lined up underneath each other, this should cause no difficulty. For example:

```
     3.5
   12.07           23.37
     .35         −  2.15
   15.92           21.22
```

5

## Multiplication

In multiplying decimals, you must remember that the decimal places in the product will be the sum of the decimal places involved in the numbers that you are multiplying. What that means in English is that if you multiply a number with three decimal places by a number with two decimal places, your product will have five decimal places (3 + 2 = 5). For example:

$$
\begin{array}{r}
5.302 \\
\times 2.21 \\
\hline
5302 \\
10604\phantom{0} \\
10604\phantom{00} \\
\hline
11.71742
\end{array}
$$

## Division

When doing division of decimals, you perform the division in the usual manner, after the following three steps:

1.  Eliminate the decimal places in the number you are dividing by, by moving the decimal point the necessary number of places to the right.

2.  In the number you are dividing, move the decimal point the *same* number of spaces to the right (add 0's if necessary).

3.  Transfer the decimal point to the line on which your answer will appear.

For example:

$$2.3 \overline{)28.06} = \qquad 2.3. \overline{)28.0.6} = \qquad
\begin{array}{r}
12.2\phantom{0} \\
23 \overline{)280.6} \\
\underline{23}\phantom{0.00} \\
50\phantom{0} \\
\underline{46}\phantom{0} \\
4\,6 \\
\underline{4\,6} \\
0
\end{array}$$

## PERCENTAGES

A third way of representing parts of units is in the form of percentages. If you remember that "per cent" means "out of one-hundred," then it should be clear that whenever we are dealing with percentages, we are dealing with hundredths. We can add and subtract percentages, but before we can do anything else with percentages (such as multiply or divide), we must change them into either fractions or decimals.

## CONVERSIONS

Since percentages, decimals, and fractions are all ways of expressing parts of a whole, we are able to convert one to the other. We do this all the time with money, for example, where we frequently call 25c "one quarter", or call $.50 "a half". (No — this is not the time to ask for the derivation of the term "two bits"!)

Basically, conversions may be carried out as follows:

### Percentages to Decimals

We have said that percent means hundredths; therefore, to convert percent to decimals, you merely need to put the decimal point in the right place. For example:

$$35\% = .35$$
$$56.8\% = .568$$

### Decimals to Percentages

Here we take the opposite route. In effect, we multiply by 100 or move the decimal point two places to the right. For example:

$$.27 = 27\%$$
$$.178 = 17.8\%$$

### Decimals to Fractions

These are most easily converted if you just put down what you read in the form of a fraction, and then reduce the fraction. For example:

$$.15 = \frac{15}{100} = \frac{3}{20}$$

$$.136 = \frac{136}{1000} = \frac{17}{125}$$

With mixed numbers, just hold the whole number on the side and proceed with the rest. For example:

$$3.628 = 3\frac{628}{1000} = 3\frac{157}{250}$$

**Fractions to Decimals**

In order to convert fractions to decimals, you actually have to do the division indicated. For example:

$$\frac{3}{4} = \text{means 3 divided by 4 or } \quad 4\overline{)3.00} = .75$$

$$\begin{array}{r} .75 \\ 4\overline{)3.00} \\ \underline{2\ 8} \\ 20 \\ \underline{20} \\ 0 \end{array}$$

$$\frac{12}{17} = \begin{array}{r} .7058+ \\ 17\overline{)12.0000} \\ \underline{11\ 9} \\ 100 \\ \underline{85} \\ 150 \\ \underline{136} \\ 14 \end{array}$$

With mixed numbers, hold the whole number on the side but *remember to put it back* in the end. For example:

$$27\frac{19}{25} = 27 \text{ (hold it!)} + \frac{19}{25}$$

$$\begin{array}{r} .76 \\ 25\overline{)19.00} \\ \underline{17\ 5} \\ 1\ 50 \end{array} \quad \text{now put back the 27}$$

$$27\frac{19}{25} = 27.76$$

Please remember: *always divide the denominator into the numerator.*

## SQUARES AND SQUARE ROOTS

### Squares

The square of a number is the number multiplied by itself. For example:

$$5^2 = 5 \times 5 = 25$$

PLEASE NOTE: it does not mean 5 x 2.

Similarly, $5^3 = 5 \times 5 \times 5 = 125$.

## Square Roots

The square root of a number is that number which when squared results in the original number. Square root is expressed by the symbol $\sqrt{\phantom{xxxx}}$ . For example:

$$\sqrt{25} = 5, \text{ because } 5 \times 5 = 25$$

You will find a table of squares and square roots at the back of this book, so that you will not have to bother playing lengthy games with square roots. It is helpful to remember the concept, however, so that you can at times approximate what the square root of a number is. For example:

$$\sqrt{75} = ?$$

Just by trial and error, we can see that $\sqrt{75}$ must be somewhere between 8 and 9 ($8^2 = 64$ and $9^2 = 81$).

## NEGATIVE NUMBERS

Until now, we have only been dealing with positive numbers; i.e., numbers that are more than or greater than zero. At times, however, we do encounter negative numbers (i.e., numbers that are less than zero). In real life, we frequently see these in the form of debts — the money we owe; maybe that's why we sometimes don't like to deal with them in statistics either. To help you overcome this problem, the following are a few simple rules that might help.

### Addition

When all the numbers you are adding are negative, simply add them in the usual way and put a minus sign in front of the sum. For example:

$$(-5) + (-7) + (-18) = -30$$

When the numbers you are adding are mixed, and there are only two of them, just subtract the smaller number from the larger number and give the result the sign of the larger number. For example:

$$(-7) + 9 = 2 \qquad (-9) + 7 = -2 \qquad 32 + (-12) = 20 \qquad (-32) + 12 = -20$$

When there are more than two numbers and the signs are all mixed up, add all of the positive ones first, then add all of the negative ones, and finally combine the results as we have done before. For example:

$$(-7) + 9 + 32 + (-12) + 23 + (-15) = 64 + (-34) = 30$$

$$(-18) + (-23) + 4 + 27 + (-26) = 31 + (-67) = -36$$

9

## Subtraction

To subtract a negative number from another number, change its sign to positive, and proceed as you did in addition. You might want to remember the grammatical rule that a "double negative" really means a positive. For example:

$$15 - (-7) = 15 + 7 = 22 \qquad\qquad 46 - (-12) = 46 + 12 = 58$$

$$(-23) - (-15) = (-23) + 15 = -8$$

## Multiplication and Division

In both the multiplication and the division of two numbers, if the signs of the two numbers are the same (either both positive or both negative), the result has a positive sign. If the signs of the two numbers are not the same (one is positive and the other negative), the result is negative. For example:

$$6 \times 7 = 42 \qquad (-6) \times (-7) = 42 \qquad 6 \times (-7) = -42 \qquad (-6) \times 7 = -42$$

$$\frac{30}{5} = 6 \qquad\qquad \frac{-30}{-5} = 6 \qquad\qquad \frac{30}{-5} = -6 \qquad\qquad \frac{-30}{5} = -6$$

When dealing with more than two numbers, or with a combination of multiplication and division, don't panic; just handle it two numbers and one operation at a time, following the above rule. For example:

$$4 \times (-8) \times 2 = (-32) \times 2 = -64$$

$$4 \times (-8) \times (-2) = (-32) \times (-2) = 64$$

$$\frac{4 \times (-10)}{8} = \frac{-40}{8} = -5$$

$$\frac{4 \times (-10)}{-8} = \frac{-40}{-8} = 5$$

$$\frac{4 \times 10}{-8} = \frac{40}{-8} = -5$$

## NUMBERS IN FORMULAS

There is nothing mysterious about formulas. If you know what each letter in the formula stands for, you can then merrily go along substituting the appropriate numbers for the letters in the formula. For example:

$$t = \frac{S - R}{\sqrt{\dfrac{S^2 + R^2 - 2RS}{N - 1}}}$$

$$S = 15$$
$$R = 5$$
$$N = 26$$

Therefore,

$$t = \frac{15 - 5}{\sqrt{\dfrac{15^2 + 5^2 - (2 \times 15 \times 5)}{26 - 1}}}$$

$$t = \frac{10}{\sqrt{\dfrac{225 + 25 - 150}{25}}}$$

$$t = \frac{10}{\sqrt{\dfrac{100}{25}}}$$

$$t = \frac{10}{\sqrt{4}}$$

$$t = \frac{10}{2}$$

$$t = 5$$

## SHORT CUTS
### Multiplying by 10, 100, 1000, etc.

Merely add the corresponding number of 0's; or, when dealing with a decimal, move the decimal point the appropriate number of places to the right. For example:

$$256 \times 100 = 25{,}600$$
$$3.789 \times 100 = 378.9$$

**Dividing by 10, 100, 1000, etc.**

Move the decimal point the appropriate number of spaces to the left. For example:

$$256 \div 100 = 2.56$$
$$57.32 \div 100 = .5732$$

With the basics dealt with in this Chapter, you should be able to do any of the calculations required in this course. For those of you for whom this review has been an insult to your intelligence and integrity, I apologize; for the other 99 percent, I hope it has been helpful.

# PRACTICE SHEETS

1. Add the following:

   a) $\frac{3}{5} + \frac{1}{6}$      b) $\frac{3}{4} + \frac{7}{8}$

   c) $\frac{3}{4} + \frac{2}{3} + \frac{5}{6}$      d) $\frac{3}{8} + \frac{1}{3} + \frac{2}{5} + \frac{5}{6}$

   e) $2\frac{5}{8} + 1\frac{1}{4} + 2\frac{7}{9}$      f) $3\frac{1}{2} + 2\frac{3}{8} + 15\frac{1}{3}$

2. Subtract:

   a) $\frac{1}{2} - \frac{3}{8}$      b) $\frac{4}{5} - \frac{2}{3}$

   c) $3\frac{5}{7} - 2\frac{16}{21}$      d) $12\frac{9}{10} - 7\frac{3}{4}$

3. Multiply:

   a) $\frac{3}{5} \times \frac{1}{6} \times \frac{3}{4} \times \frac{2}{3}$      b) $\frac{3}{4} \times \frac{7}{8} \times \frac{3}{8} \times \frac{1}{3} \times \frac{5}{6}$

   c) $2\frac{3}{4} \times 3\frac{2}{3} \times \frac{1}{2}$      d) $2\frac{5}{8} \times 3\frac{1}{2} \times 2\frac{3}{8} \times \frac{1}{4}$

4. Divide:

   a) $\frac{3}{4} \div \frac{7}{8}$      b) $\frac{4}{5} \div \frac{2}{3}$

   c) $2\frac{1}{2} \div 3\frac{5}{6}$      d) $6\frac{2}{3} \div 2\frac{1}{3}$

5. Fill in the equivalent terms:

| | Fractions | Decimals | Percentages |
|---|---|---|---|
| a) | $\frac{12}{17}$ | | |
| b) | | .48 | |
| c) | | | 36% |
| d) | $\frac{15}{19}$ | | |
| e) | | .79 | |
| f) | | | 52.8% |
| g) | $\frac{7}{8}$ | | |
| h) | | .234 | |
| i) | | | 36.52% |
| j) | $\frac{112}{243}$ | | |

*(continued on next page)*

|  | Fractions | Decimals | Percentages |
|---|---|---|---|
| k) |  | 3.176 |  |
| l) |  |  | .07% |
| m) | $4\frac{2}{3}$ |  |  |
| n) |  | 2.375 |  |
| o) |  |  | .32% |

6. Using the Table in the Appendix, please answer the following:

a) $(1.96)^2 =$

b) $(7.32)^2 =$

c) $(26.3)^2 =$

d) $(64.8)^2 =$

e) $(3.10)^2 =$

f) $(827)^2 =$

g) $(47.99)^2 =$

h) $(327.42)^2 =$

i) $(2.4683)^2 =$

j) $(4,876.58)^2 =$

k) $\sqrt{1.85} =$

l) $\sqrt{8.832} =$

m) $\sqrt{16.54} =$

n) $\sqrt{89.12} =$

o) $\sqrt{237.8} =$

p) $\sqrt{750.3} =$

q) $\sqrt{3,000} =$

r) $\sqrt{6,456} =$

s) $\sqrt{8,251.52} =$

t) $\sqrt{9,476.12} =$

7. Do what you're told!

a) $23 + (-5) + (-12) - 6 + (-15) + 72 =$

b) $(-15) - (-12) + 32 - 5 - (-27) =$

c) $(3) \times (-5) \times 6 \times (-7) =$

d) $\dfrac{(4) \times (-6)}{(12) \times (-3)} =$

e) $\dfrac{32 - (-5) + (-7)}{(2)\,(-3)\,(-4)} =$

f) $\dfrac{[(57)\,(-6)] + 3}{[(-14)\,(3)] + 8} - 2$

g) $\dfrac{(25)\,(2)}{(13)\,(-34)} - [(63)\,(-3)]$

8.  a)  Given:  W = 10   N = 100   A = 910   B = 125

$$S = W \sqrt{\frac{A}{N} - \left(\frac{B}{N}\right)^2}$$

Solve for S.

b)  Given:  N = 20   X = 40   Y = 15

$$Q = \frac{N(XY) - (X+Y)}{\sqrt{(NX^2 - Y^2)(NY^2 - X^2)}}$$

Solve for Q.

c)  Given:  N = 15   S = 6   M = 13   r = 4

$$T = 2 \sqrt{\frac{(N-1)S^2 + (M-1)r^2}{N + M - 2}}$$

Solve for T.

# CHAPTER 3
# BASIC CONCEPTS

Now that you are totally proficient in all kinds of complicated mathematical computations and manipulations, we can spend some time discussing a few basic concepts that are essential for understanding research and statistics. You are undoubtedly familiar with some of these from your previous readings in research; furthermore, many of these same concepts are used by everyone in everyday life. What we shall attempt to do here, however, is to emphasize their statistical meaning, while continuously relating back to their usual everyday meaning. In some ways, then, this is almost like a study of vocabulary words in some foreign language: the definitions are important because, obviously, we must all end up speaking the same language. In many ways, the definitions are over-simplified, and we refer you to a research text for further elucidation. The different concepts follow below:

## NUMBERS

You all know what numbers are — things like 5, 10, and 436.298. The important thing to remember in statistics is that these numbers, and all numbers, are in and of themselves meaningless. Numbers only have that meaning which is given to them by the process that produces them. Numbers by themselves are not the real world and have no meaning in the real world. For example, five does not mean anything unless you at least tell me five what (or whats). Are we talking about five seconds, five years, five hours, or five centuries?

Two extreme illustrations to help you remember this point:

We could collect everyone's telephone number in a given class — 298-7955, 239-3669, 426-9563, etc., and calculate an average telephone number. This would obviously be a totally useless exercise and the resulting number, although indeed representing the average telephone number in that class, would be totally without meaning in the real world.

According to the sages of "Playboy," "Penthouse," and "Hustler," the ideal measurements for a woman are 37-24-34, or very close to that. To their rather limited minds and perspectives, these are the embodiments of a creature delightful to behold. If we would try to describe their ideal to them by saying that the average measurement of this woman is 31.667 inches (which indeed it is), it is obvious that we would have destroyed for them the meaning of the original measurements. Indeed, that same average measurement might have originated from a man, whose measurements are 32-32-31.

I am sure that all of you—with your fertile imaginations—can come up with numerous other such examples, where a simple statistical manipulation destroys the meaning of the data.

I think that this point is sufficiently clear without having to belabor it any further. The reason for this introductory caution is that researchers, statisticians, professors, and even students sometimes become so caught up in this world of numbers, that they forget the simple truth which we have illustrated above. Throughout, then, it is important that you do not just "play games" with numbers, but that you understand the purpose of playing these games, and make sure that the net result of manipulating the numbers has some real meaning.

## VARIABLES

Research has, at times, been described as the study of variables. It is therefore important that we clarify at the outset what variables are, and what the different types of variables are with which we will be dealing.

Basically, (watch out — here comes a definition!) a variable is something that varies. In other words, it is anything that is different from time to time or from case to case. This includes just about all phenomena of the known world. What is not included are the kinds of things that, under normal conditions and normal circumstances, we assume not to vary. For example, a study of the number of eyes or number of noses would be pathetically ridiculous, because in normal populations of human beings, number of eyes and number of noses usually do not vary. When you think of a variable, then, you have to be able to visualize at least two possible values of that variable; as long as you can do that, you can call it a variable.

Now variables themselves also vary. There are basically four types of variables: nominal, ordinal, interval, and ratio. We shall now discuss each of these in some detail.

### Nominal Variables

A nominal variable is one which calls somebody a name (that is why it is called a nominal variable). Another term frequently used is categorical variable, by which we mean that this is the kind of variable that helps us categorize the subjects of our study. For example, some nominal variables are race, national origin, sex (male or female, not frequency, you understand), hair color, and religion. In all of these variables you are calling somebody a name; you are labeling them; you are categorizing them. The variable of national origin, for example, might be divided into English, Irish, Scottish, Mexican, German, Polish, Russian, etc. The variable of religion may be divided into Protestant, Catholic, Jewish, Buddhist, Zoroastrian, etc.

One can also take a variable and look at it from the viewpoint of what is sometimes called a none/some variable. If we are interested, for example, in comparing the views of Catholics with the views of non-Catholics, we might merely look at the variable of religion in terms of Catholicism or non-Catholicism, and thus will put Jews, Protestants, Buddhists, and even Zoroastrians into this non-Catholic group. When we do this (i.e., when we view a variable from a none/some viewpoint), we sometimes refer to it as a dichotomy.

### Ordinal Variables

An ordinal variable is one in which the values of the variable are ordered. We are speaking here of the kinds of variables that measure the degree of something. For example, if we look at the variable of height, we can view this variable on the basis of a scale going from small to medium to tall; or, we might wish to measure the degree of students' satisfaction with their statistics class on a scale ranging from "totally satisfactory," to "satisfactory," to "eh," to "unsatisfactory," to "execrable." Similarly, we could rank students in size order and call the tallest student number one, the next to the tallest number two, the next to the next to the tallest number three, etc. We would then end up with these students being in some kind of order, and would thus have an ordinal variable (size) that we are dealing with. It should be emphasized that, although the values of an ordinal variable are in order, the distances between the values are not necessarily the same. For example, in rank ordering students by size, the tallest student may be 6'4", the next one 6'2" (obviously a difference of two inches), while the third student may be 5'8" (a difference here of 6 inches). Similarly, when you stop to think of it, the "distance" between "totally satisfied" and "satisfied" may not be the same distance as the distance between "eh" and "satisfied." The important point to remember is that viewing a variable from an ordinal standpoint does not guarantee equal distances between its values.

### Interval Variables

In an interval variable, the intervals between the different values of the variable are the same. In other words, in this kind of variable, the distances between the different conceivable values of the variable are all alike. Taking temperature, as measured on a Fahrenheit scale, for example, we are dealing with a standard interval (one degree), which remains the same throughout. Thus the difference between 10 and 20 degrees is the same as the difference between 70 and 80 degrees. Please note, however, that it does not really make sense to say that 80°F is twice as hot as (or has twice the temperature of) 40°F. The problem here is that on the Fahrenheit scale, we do not have an absolute zero point. This will hopefully become clearer when we turn to ratio variables. So let's do that.

### Ratio Variables

Here, at last, we have all the admirable qualities of interval variables plus a logical absolute zero point. Taking age in years, for example, we are not only dealing with a standard interval (one year), but also with the logical notion that no one is less than 0 years old. Similarly, when we deal with income in dollars, we can assume that it can not be less than $0.00. Note that in these cases we can say that a 40 year old person is really twice as old as a 20 year old; and that someone earning $30,000 per year is indeed making three times as much as someone with an income of $10,000 per year. We are speaking here, of course, purely from a statistical viewpoint. $2,000 certainly mean much more to an individual currently earning $5,000 per year than the same $2,000 mean to someone earning $50,000 per year; but from a statistical perspective, the $2,000 are the same.

### VALUES OF VARIABLES

We have already used the term "values" in this discussion of variables, and I hope that it is relatively clear. The values of a variable are the actual measuring points which are used to measure the variable. Thus, in a study of hair color, the values of the variable might be black, brunette, blond, red-head, etc. In a study of marital status, the values of the variable might be single, married, divorced, separated, widowed. What should be noted is that with any kind of variable, the values of that variable may be stated in many different ways, and there is no "right" or "wrong" way. It all depends upon the purpose of your study. For example, let us take the variable of age to illustrate this point. In a study of infant mortality, you might wish to use days as the values of your variable, and might be interested in finding out whether the infants under study died at the age of one day, two days, three days, etc. If, on the other hand, you are doing a study of developmental stages in young children, you might wish to use months as the values of your variable. With a study dealing with adults, the values of your variable might well be in years, or even in five or ten-year intervals. A study to determine the impact that the lowering of voting age has had upon the coming elections might deal with the variable "age" only in the following values: 18-21 and over 21. Essentially, the point we are trying to make is that before you can determine how you are going to handle your variable, you must have clearly in mind what it is that you really want to find out. Studying infant mortality in terms of years of age is as stupid as studying voting patterns in terms of days of age.

Generally, it is advisable to collect data with the values as precise and detailed as possible—at the most advanced level of measurement possible. In other words, if you have collected your data regarding age at the ratio level (i.e., age at last birthday), you can play all kinds of statistical games. If you like, you can even decide to move from the ratio level to the ordinal level, by classifying the data into categories of "young," "middle-aged," and "old." Note that if you had collected the data at this ordinal level, it would not be possible for you to translate them to the ratio level — you would be stuck at the ordinal level for life.

For any variable, the categories used should be mutually exclusive (i.e., they must not overlap), and, taken all together, they must be all inclusive (i.e., together they must account for all possible values of the variable). It is obviously confusing to a 30 year old to know where to place himself when faced with the two categories "20-30 years" and "30-40 years." Conversely, where does an Asian-American go to register when faced with a categorization of "White," "Black," and "Brown"? Even when you think that you have exhausted all possibilities in stating the values of your variable, it may still be a good idea to add a category such as "other" to make absolutely sure that all possibilities are accounted for.

## THE SIGNIFICANCE OF THE TYPES OF VARIABLES

Categorizing variables into nominal, ordinal, interval, and ratio variables is not merely done for exercise, but has considerable significance in terms of what one can actually do with the data. With a nominal variable, one can really do no more than state a frequency distribution and/or a percentage distribution. For example, if we find that 60 percent of the students at State University are female and 40 percent are male, that is about as far as we go. It would make no sense to say that the "average student" is 6/10 female and 4/10 male. It is even difficult to imagine such a student. Similarly, if we are dealing with ethnic groups and come to the conclusion that our population is 50 percent White, 20 percent Black, 20 percent Hispanic, and 10 percent Oriental, it makes no sense to try and describe the "average" individual. Thus, whenever we have a nominal variable, the best we can do is use some relatively basic descriptive statistics.

When we move to ordinal variables, it becomes possible to use some other statistical descriptions such as cumulative percentages or frequencies. Most researchers and statisticians are willing to take a five-point scale, such as very good-good-adequate-poor-very poor, and assign point values to the scale from 1 to 5 and then perform all kinds of statistical manipulations with the results. Actually, this is relatively "kosher," as long as we do not then interpret the data as indicating that someone with a score of 2 is twice as good (or half as good) as someone with a score of 4; that is, we can not say that "good" is twice as good as "poor," or that "very good" is five times as good as "very poor." What we can say, however, in interpreting such data, is that "good" is better than "poor" and that "very good" is certainly better than "very poor."

Variables that form an interval scale, and especially those that form a ratio scale, can be manipulated in a vast variety of ways and still give us statistically valid results. As has been pointed out, $4,000 really is twice as much as $2,000, and 75 years of age really is three times as much as 25 years of age. It is with interval and ratio data, then, that one is able, with totally clear conscience, to speak of means, standard deviations, and all other kinds of delightful things with which you will shortly become very conversant. It should be noted that so-called "non-parametric" statistics can be used with many different types of variables; but don't worry about that — yet.

## STATISTICAL POPULATION
Following through on our simplistic definitions, we should say that populations refer to people. But watch out, because this is an exception. Usually when we speak of populations, we do mean people. Statistically, however, when we speak of a statistical population, we mean all the values of a variable for a certain group. For example, if we are interested in the income of students at State University, our statistical population would consist of the values of that variable, and might include $2,000, $14,000, $7,000, $12,000, etc. It is these values of the variable which make up our statistical population.

## AN ANT'S--EYE VIEW OF THIS CHAPTER
1. **Numbers:** only have the meaning assigned to them by the process that produces them.

2. **Variables:** something that varies.

   a) Nominal:     calling a name; e.g., Republican, Democrat, Independent, other.
   b) Ordinal:     in order by degree; e.g., very good, good, bad, very bad.
   c) Interval:     intervals between values are the same.
   d) Ratio:     also have an absolute zero point; e.g., age in years; can be statistically manipulated in many ways.

3. **Values of Variables:** depend upon what you want to know.

4. **Statistical Population:** all the values of the variable.

# PRACTICE SHEET

1. State whether the following variables are nominal, ordinal, interval, or ratio; then give several possible values of the variable.

   a) Types of cases handled by XYZ Family Service Agency.
   b) Major problems manifested by clients of Protective Services for the Aged.
   c) Severity of general deterioration of clients of same agency.
   d) Level of economic competence for residents of Ocean Beach.
   e) Time spent in direct contact with clients in Drug Education Programs in San York County.

2. For the following, indicate the type of variable:

   a) Education. Categories are: elementary school, junior high, high school, college, graduate school.
   b) Attendance. Categories are: frequently, sometimes, never.
   c) Undergraduate college. Categories are: University of California, California State College, Adelphi University, other.
   d) Residence. Categories are: New York, other.

3. Choose one variable, and illustrate how this same variable might be measured at the nominal, ordinal, and interval levels.

4. As makes obvious good sense to everyone, the categories into which any variable is divided should be mutually exclusive and, taken all together, they must be all inclusive. For the following, state whether or not the categories of each of the variables meet these requirements. If you find some boo-boos, state what is wrong and fix it up.

   a) Age of patients at County Hospital (in years): 0-2, 3-5, 6-10, 11-20, 21-45, 45-65, 66-80.
   b) Major types of publications: professional journals, newspapers, Life Magazine, paperbacks, Playboy, popular periodicals, underground publications.
   c) Classification of U.S. coins: penny, nickel, dime, quarter, half-dollar, dollar, other.
   d) Weight of female students at State University (in pounds): less than 90, 90-100, 101-105, 106-110, 110-115, 116-120, 120-125, 125-130, 131-140, 141-150, 151-170, 171-200, over 200.
   e) Ability of retarded children to feed selves: not able, partially able, completely able.
   f) Types of services received by clients: protective services only, supportive services only, preventive services only, some combination of above.

# CHAPTER 4
# ORGANIZING YOUR DATA

Actually, the idea of considering the organization of your data only after you have collected them is rather silly. Ideally, you should have planned ahead for the organization of your data before you even started collecting the data and should have designed your instrument in such a way that this step (organization of data) becomes quite simple. But assuming that you did not have all this knowledge (or else, why are you reading this book?), we will now try to fill in some of these gaps.

Basically, the purpose of organizing your data in some manner is so that you can understand it, and so that you can present it to the reader with some clarity. With all presentations of data, the most important criterion is whether or not the meaning of the material being presented is clear. We try to achieve this in a variety of ways — through textual material, charts, graphs, nude centerpage fold-outs, etc. Most frequently, however, statistical material is presented in the form of charts or tables, and it is upon this kind of presentation that this chapter concentrates. Please note that since the goal is clarity of meaning, there are no absolute standards or rules, and there are no absolute "right" or "wrong" ways of presenting the data — it's all a question of what you are trying to convey, and to whom you are trying to convey it.

Another way of looking at the purpose of tables is to compare them to illustrations in a book of fiction. The illustrations are used to *illustrate* the textual material, not to replace it. Similarly, tables cannot stand by themselves in a study. They must be discussed in the text of the study, and in fact, should only appear when they help to clarify, explain, or illustrate the textual material.

## NOMINAL VARIABLES
Let us start with a simple nominal variable such as sex, and let us assume that you have done a thorough study of 10 individuals to determine whether they are male or female. Your raw data may look as follows:

male     male     male     female     female     male     female     male     female     male

Obviously, this listing of the values of the variable is not very useful, and certainly if we have more individuals or a variable with a greater number of values, this method would very quickly become unmanageable. Our next step, therefore, is to group the data. This is done most simply by using tally marks. The above data would be grouped as follows:

Male       *HH* /
Female     ////

We could present these data in the form of a simple table by noting the frequency distribution of males and females in this group of 10. All that frequency distribution means, by the way, is the frequency with which a variable is distributed amongst the different categories. We could, therefore, set up a frequency distribution which would look as follows:

| Sex | Frequency |
|------|-----------|
| Male | 6 |
| Female | 4 |
| **Total** | 10 |

Or we could present the data somewhat differently:

| Male | Female | Total |
|------|--------|-------|
| 6 | 4 | 10 |

The basic purpose of grouping our data, of course, is to make them more understandable and to make them clear at a glance. It is frequently more meaningful to represent these kinds of data in terms of ratios, proportions, or percentages. We could ask, for example, what the ratio is of males to females. The answer is that the ratio of males to females = $\frac{males}{females}$, which = $\frac{6}{4}$ = 1.5 to 1. What this means is that there are $1\frac{1}{2}$ males to every female. Sometimes, in an attempt to express this in terms of hundreds, we then multiply by 100 to say that the ratio of males to females is 150 to 100, which is still the same ratio, of course.

We can also express this in terms of a proportion. What proportion of individuals were males? The proportion of males = $\frac{males}{total}$, which = $\frac{6}{10}$ = $\frac{3}{5}$ or .6. The proportion of females = $\frac{females}{total}$ = $\frac{4}{10}$ = $\frac{2}{5}$ or .4. In other words, $\frac{3}{5}$ or .6 of the total were male, while $\frac{2}{5}$ or .4 of the total were female. We could further translate the data into percentages, in which case, of course, we would do the same divisions we did for proportions and arrive at the astounding notion that 60 percent of our group were male and 40 percent were female.

I hope you realize that the underlying purpose in speaking of ratios, proportions or percentages is to relate what we found to some kind of standard base. Six males are relatively meaningless until we can say six males out of how many; or six males in comparison to how many females; or what the ratio of males is to females; or what percentage of the total population was male and what percentage was female.

At times, we are interested in more than one variable at a time. For example, we might wish to know the sex distribution of students at several institutions of higher learning in San Diego. Essentially, then, we are dealing with two variables — sex and schools. The results of a study of a sample of students from San Diego State University (SDSU), University of California at San Diego (UCSD), and University of San Diego (USD) might be summarized as follows:

|        | Male  | Female | Total |
|--------|-------|--------|-------|
| SDSU   | 900   | 1,100  | 2,000 |
| UCSD   | 1,500 | 1,000  | 2,500 |
| USD    | 600   | 700    | 1,300 |
| Total  | 3,000 | 2,800  | 5,800 |

The data in this table could be interpreted in a variety of ways. It indicates, for example, that there are slightly more female students than male students at SDSU and at USD, while there are considerably more males than females at UCSD. We could further say that the ratio of males to females at UCSD was 1500/1000, which = 1.5 to 1. In other words, there are 1½ males to every female at UCSD. We could also note that the proportion of males at SDSU was 900/2000, which = 9/20, which = .45 or 45 percent, and the proportion of females at USD is 700/1300, which = 7/13, which is approximately 53.8 percent.

We might also, of course, look at the data the other way around and ask: Out of the total of 3,000 males in our sample, what percentage came from SDSU, and what percentage came from UCSD and USD? We could ask a similar question regarding the females and look at the totals from the same view point. I hope that what this indicates to you is that different percentages can be obtained, depending upon the base figure. The base figure is that total figure which adds up to 100 percent. So here, again, to say that we have 45 percent males is meaningless, unless we specify the base of that figure and say that at San Diego State University 45 percent of the students are male (it is understood here that our base is the total number of students at San Diego State University).

We can complicate matters further by introducing still another variable. Let us say that I am interested in determining the sex and marital status of students at the same three colleges. When I have finished collecting the data, I could present them in a table which looks as follows:

|        | Male | | | Female | | | |
|        | Single | Married | Total | Single | Married | Total | TOTAL |
|--------|--------|---------|-------|--------|---------|-------|-------|
| SDSU   | 700    | 200     | 900   | 800    | 300     | 1,100 | 2,000 |
| UCSD   | 1,000  | 500     | 1,500 | 700    | 300     | 1,000 | 2,500 |
| USD    | 500    | 100     | 600   | 600    | 100     | 700   | 1,300 |
| Total  | 2,200  | 800     | 3,000 | 2,100  | 700     | 2,800 | 5,800 |

On this table, percentages can be calculated on an even greater number of total bases. For example, we could figure percentages on a sex base, on a college total base, and on a marital status base. We could, of course, always figure things on the basis of a total total base. But, lest we be accused of stuttering or of typographical errors, I shall attempt to refrain from using such terms as "total totals."

It is usually not advisable to complicate the presentation of data by introducing too many variables in the same table. Please remember that the underlying purpose of tables is to present the data clearly and understandably, rather than to obfuscate.

Aside from frequency distributions, ratios, proportions, and the use of percentages, there is really only one other way in which nominal data can be described, and that is through the use of the modal category. We will discuss the mode later as one of the measures of central tendency, but for the time being, let us just say that the mode is that category which has the greatest frequency. For example, if we are doing a study of marital status of students broken down into much finer categories than we have thus far dealt with, we might find the following results:

| | |
|---|---:|
| Single, never married | 850 |
| Married and living with spouse | 250 |
| Married, not living with spouse | 50 |
| Divorced | 130 |
| Legally separated but not divorced | 70 |
| Widowed | 50 |
| Total | 1,400 |

In this distribution, the modal category would be "single, never married." This is the category that contained more individuals than any other category in the study.

## ORDINAL VARIABLES

As we have stated before, an ordinal variable deals with order. It is the kind of variable that basically says that A is greater than B, which is greater than C, which is greater than D, etc.; or that one thing is better than another. With such variables it sometimes becomes important to try to answer the question of how many cases are better than or worse than a given value. In order to enable us to do this more easily, we sometimes present such data in the form of cumulative frequencies. Very simply, a cumulative frequency distribution is one in which we allow the frequencies to accumulate. In other words, we just keep adding them up. For example, let us say that we would like to look at the results of a study of grades given to a total of 50 students in a course entitled "Non-Parametric Statistics as Applied to Parametric Population Proportions." It was found that 6 students received the grade of A, 14 students received the grade of B, 20 students received a grade of C, 6 students received a grade of D and 4 students a grade of F (poor souls). If we present these data in our usual frequency distribution, the table looks as follows:

| Grade | f |
|---|---:|
| A | 6 |
| B | 14 |
| C | 20 |
| D | 6 |
| F | 4 |
| Total | 50 |

If we now want to construct a table of cumulative frequency, we can merely start at the bottom, and add up the frequencies we have already enumerated. In other words, we can say that 4 students received a grade of F. Adding those 4 to the 6 who received a grade of D gives us 10, and we can therefore say that 10 students received a grade of D or worse. Similarly, we can then get 30 students who received a grade of C or worse (4F + 6D + 20C). A table presenting both the original frequency and the cumulative frequency looks as follows:

| Grade | f | Cumulative Frequency |
|-------|-----|----------------------|
| A | 6 | 50 |
| B | 14 | 44 |
| C | 20 | 30 |
| D | 6 | 10 |
| F | 4 | 4 |
| Total | 50 | — |

Looking at this kind of a table, it becomes very easy to note at a glance that, for example, 44 students out of the 50 received the grade of B or worse. Similarly, we could calculate percentages of these frequencies, and if we cumulate the percentages we would end up with what is called the percentile. Using the same data but translating the frequency distribution into percentages looks as follows:

| Grade | f | Percentage |
|-------|-----|------------|
| A | 6 | 12 |
| B | 14 | 28 |
| C | 20 | 40 |
| D | 6 | 12 |
| F | 4 | 8 |
| Total | 50 | 100% |

Cumulating these percentages exactly as we did with the original frequency would result in the following percentile distribution:

| Grade | Percentage | Percentile |
|-------|------------|------------|
| A | 12 | 100 |
| B | 28 | 88 |
| C | 40 | 60 |
| D | 12 | 20 |
| F | 8 | 8 |
| Total | 100 | — |

We can thus see that a student receiving a B, for example, is at the 88th percentile. This means that 88 percent of the students did as poorly as he did or worse, and consequently 12 percent did better that he did. Similarly, if you take an exam and are told that your score was at the 98th percentile, this means that you scored comparatively well — very well in fact, because note that this means that only 2 percent of the students taking that particular test did better that you did. The use of percentiles enables us to present more clearly the way in which a certain score or a certain value of an ordinal variable compares with the entire distribution.

## INTERVAL AND RATIO VARIABLES

In dealing with data derived from interval or ratio variables, we frequently end up with huge lists of raw data, and the question then arises as to how one can best present these data in such a way that they become most meaningful to the reader. Examples in the literature abound, and the one that I have recently become very fond of is the measure of "Times to the Nearest Tenth Second for 151 Albino Rats Running a Straight Alley".[1] But since this illustration is not totally relevant to the social sciences and has racist overtones besides, we will not use it. Instead, as an example of how quantitative data are organized, let us use the number of months that a sample of 70 families have been on AFDC.[2] The raw data look as follows:

| 52  | 48 | 4  | 46  | 7   | 36 | 1   |
|-----|----|----|-----|-----|----|-----|
| 60  | 80 | 4  | 49  | 74  | 6  | 1   |
| 3   | 34 | 8  | 42  | 205 | 5  | 4   |
| 75  | 27 | 4  | 58  | 216 | 3  | 7   |
| 50  | 29 | 8  | 59  | 34  | 8  | 6   |
| 120 | 47 | 8  | 47  | 18  | 8  | 49  |
| 60  | 38 | 9  | 200 | 30  | 1  | 43  |
| 24  | 7  | 45 | 8   | 160 | 7  | 156 |
| 18  | 6  | 20 | 4   | 28  | 5  | 11  |
| 96  | 7  | 50 | 8   | 52  | 1  | 15  |

Obviously, the raw data here are relatively useless. We might note that some values are as low as one month; others are as high as 200, 205, and even 216 months. But just looking at the raw data makes any other statements almost impossible.

In order to further clarify what it is we are dealing with, we shall move on to arrange the data in the form of an array. This involves arranging the values in order from low to high, and the result is as follows:

| 1 | 4 | 7  | 15 | 34 | 49 | 74  |
|---|---|----|----|----|----|-----|
| 1 | 5 | 8  | 18 | 36 | 49 | 75  |
| 1 | 5 | 8  | 18 | 38 | 50 | 80  |
| 1 | 6 | 8  | 20 | 42 | 50 | 96  |
| 3 | 6 | 8  | 24 | 43 | 52 | 120 |
| 3 | 6 | 8  | 27 | 43 | 52 | 156 |
| 4 | 7 | 8  | 28 | 46 | 58 | 160 |
| 4 | 7 | 8  | 29 | 47 | 59 | 200 |
| 4 | 7 | 9  | 30 | 47 | 60 | 205 |
| 4 | 7 | 11 | 34 | 48 | 60 | 216 |

Here we can at least begin to see the emergence of some pattern. We can note that we have a considerable number of cases of very few months' duration (one to eight months for example); that, on the other hand, there are only three cases between 200 and 216 months. We might decide, therefore,

---

[1] Paul R. Games and George R. Klare, *Elementary Statistics* (New York: McGraw-Hill, 1967), p. 31.
[2] These data are taken from Bernice W. Polemis, *Statistics* 4th Edition, Chicago, School of Social Service Administration, 1966.

as a next step, to organize the data into a frequency distribution. Having already observed what we have observed, we agree, I hope, that it would be ridiculous to present a frequency distribution month by month. It therefore becomes necessary to lump the data into some kind of interval. If we start by grouping the data into six-month intervals, we end up with the following distribution:

| Intervals of 6 months | Number of Cases |
|---|---|
| 1 and under 6 months | 13 |
| 6 and under 12 | 17 |
| 12 and under 18 | 1 |
| 18 and under 24 | 3 |
| 24 and under 30 | 4 |
| 30 and under 36 | 3 |
| 36 and under 42 | 2 |
| 42 and under 48 | 6 |
| 48 and under 54 | 7 |
| 54 and under 60 | 2 |
| 60 and under 66 | 2 |
| 66 and under 72 | 0 |
| 72 and under 80 | 2 |
| 80 and over | 8 |
| Total | 70 |

What we can see from this kind of presentation of the data is that there is, indeed, a considerable concentration of cases during the first year, whereas there is a considerable spread in the categories beyond 12 months. In fact, had we continued our six-month intervals beyond 80 months all the way to 216 months, more than 20 additional intervals would have been necessary just to account for the last 8 cases. Most of these intervals, of course, would have no frequencies at all in them. At this point, we would have to go back to the question, "What is it that we are trying to say with these data, and how can this best be said?" Furthermore, "What do the data indicate to us?" As honest researchers, I assume that we would not wish to present the data in a purposely misleading way. What seems to be indicated from looking at the data is that a considerable number of cases have been in existence less than one year, and that should be made obvious to the reader. An almost equally large number of cases have been in existence between one and five years; and 12 cases have been in existence more than five years. We might even want to split this last group into two separate intervals in order to really clarify the "chronicity" of some of the cases. The final table might look as follows:

| Years on AFDC | f |
|---|---|
| Under 1 year | 30 |
| 1 – under 5 years | 28 |
| 5 – under 10 years | 6 |
| 10 years or more | 6 |
| Total | 70 |

28

We have presented these data here in unequal intervals, and in this case this seems necessary in order to observe some of the essential features of the data. It should be clarified that there is no "correct" way of presenting these kinds of data. All of the above presentations are equally "correct." It really becomes a question of how the data are best presented for the purpose for which we are presenting them. One might note here that some individuals, in trying to stress that families are on AFDC for relatively short periods of time, might use these data to point out that almost one half of the families (30 out of 70) have been receiving AFDC less than one year. Others, on the other hand, might use the same data to stress that families tend to stay on AFDC for extended periods of time: 41.43 percent (29 out of 70) have been on AFDC for more than three years, and almost 20 percent (12 out of 70) have been receiving AFDC for longer than five years; in fact, almost 10 percent have been on AFDC for more than 10 years; and (would you believe?) there is a family in our midst to whom our beloved State has paid AFDC for 216 months, or a total of 18 years!

All of the statements above are true and come from the same data. We hope that one of the things you will learn by the time you are finished with this book is how to intelligently question such skewed and obviously biased presentations of data.

There are a few other things that we ought to note when speaking about interval and ratio data. I hope we have clarified the point that there is no hard and fast rule for the size of the class interval. It depends upon the number of observations, the kind of data that are available, and the amount of data. At the time the data are collected, it is helpful to have as many distinctions as possible; you can then always collapse the categories if they prove to be too detailed (as we did with the data above). If, on the other hand, you start out collecting the data with only very broad categories, you might very well be obscuring some important details, and will never even realize it. Also, in terms of the size of the interval, it is helpful to the reader to use customary intervals; i.e., six-month or one year intervals, or even five year intervals. The data would obviously be more difficult to interpret if we used, let us say, eight-month intervals. Finally, it should be pointed out that even where you have zero frequencies in a category, that category cannot be skipped in the table, but must be listed with the "0" entered under "frequency." This is done to assure the reader (and yourself) that you did not just skip that category by mistake.

## THE MEANING OF CLASS INTERVALS

In essence, the meaning of the class interval (i.e., what the "real" limitations of the intervals are) is determined by the way in which the data were collected and by the characteristics of the data. With age, for example, if we asked, "What was your age on your last birthday?" then the class limitations of "5 and under 10," "10 and under 15," "15 and under 20," etc., are really extended from five years to nine years and 365 days, 10 years to 14 years and 365 days, etc. At other times, however, when we are speaking of weight, or height, or scores on a test our class interval may really extend from just below the lower limit to just above the upper limit. With such data, if we take a class interval which is labeled 100 to 105, we can assume that the numbers 99.5, 99.6, 99.7, 99.8, and 99.9 have also gone into this interval, if they occurred in the data. Similarly, the numbers 105.1, 105.2, 105.3, and 105.4 would also have been included in this interval. The interval 100 to 105 thus technically includes all numbers greater than or equal to 99.5 and less than 105.5.

Still another kind of data, such as that resulting from counting people or chairs per room, is rather absolute when categorized; that is, intervals for data of "students per class," which run: 11-15, 16-20, 21-25, etc., obviously mean just that. It would be ridiculous to imagine 15.6 students.

It is sometimes helpful in this regard to think of some measures of variables as being *discrete,* and some as being *continuous.* Age, for example, is a "continuously" measured variable, and if we merely see a table with age categories of 10-19, 20-29, 30-39, etc., we must remember that most probably the manner in which these data were collected and organized resulted in a distribution which really is categorized into 10-19.999 years, 20-29.999 years, etc. The number of students per class, on the other hand, is a "discretely" measured variable, where we don't have to worry about how the class with 19.25 students is categorized.

These distinctions become especially helpful when we come to determining the midpoint of each interval. Some further computations deal with this question of midpoint of class intervals, and it is therefore important that we clarify its meaning now. In most cases and in most tables, the midpoint is easily apparent. Thus, for example, if the class intervals for age are stated as 70-79, 80-89, 90-99, then the midpoints clearly are 75, 85, 95, because the intervals really run from 70-79.999, 80-80.999, etc. When, however, the class intervals for a discrete variable are 100-105, 106-111, and 112-117, then the midpoints of these intervals are not so apparent. The manner in which we calculate the midpoint then is to take the lower limit, and add it to the upper limit, and divide by 2. In other words, the midpoint with such data equals $\frac{L + U}{2}$ where L stands for the lower limit and U stands for the upper limit of the interval. This would mean that the midpoint for the class interval 100 to 105 is equal to:

$$\frac{100 + 105}{2} = \frac{205}{2} = 102.5$$

Similarly, the midpoint of the 112-117 class interval equals:

$$\frac{112 + 117}{2} = \frac{229}{2} = 114.5$$

## CODING

As you know, most data are collected by researchers on the basis of some kind of questionnaire or schedule. Basically, the question may be either closed or open-ended. For example, we might ask: "Do you currently live in Dubova County?" The answers might be "yes," "no," or "don't know." There are other possibilities, such as refusals, for example, but generally, this is a "closed" question with predictable limited responses. If, on the other hand, we are dealing with a question such as, "What do you like best about State University School of Social Work?" — here a whole host of responses is possible, and it would be extremely unlikely that we could predict all possible responses in advance. This, then, is clearly an open-ended question. No matter whether it is a closed or open-ended question, at some point, when all the data are collected, and you hopefully have a sizeable sample, you will have to code all the responses, so that the data can be pulled together more easily, and, perhaps, be punched onto IBM cards, enabling the computer to play with your data.

Essentially, what is meant by "coding" the data is that a number is assigned to a certain response. For our question regarding residence, we might code a "yes" as "1," a response of "no" as "5," and a "don't know" response as "9." Spreading out the coding of the responses helps to minimize error. The more questions that we can pre-code (i.e., code before the questionnaire is even administered), the easier that step of data analysis becomes. On the other hand, we must be careful only to pre-code those items for which all the possible responses are predictable; otherwise, I am sure you realize, we can end up in deep trouble. The open-ended items, which we were unable to pre-code, are finally coded at a "coding conference" after the data have been collected, and code numbers are assigned to the most common or the most significant responses; the rare ones are usually lumped under "other." To make sure that all this information is clear and can be re-interpreted after the computer gets through with it, a code book is usually constructed. The following is a sample page of my very own code book:

| Column | Variable | Coding |
|--------|----------|--------|
| 1,2 | Case Number | Identification Number; from 01 to 99 |
| 3 | Sex | 1 = male<br>5 = female<br>9 = no response |
| 4 | Age | 1 = 21–25 years<br>2 = 26–30 years<br>3 = 31–35 years<br>4 = 36–40 years<br>5 = 41–45 years<br>6 = over 45 years<br>9 = no response |
| 5 | Marital Status | 1 = single, never married<br>2 = married living with spouse<br>3 = separated<br>4 = divorced<br>5 = widowed<br>9 = no response |
| 6 | Health | 1 = very good<br>2 = good<br>3 = adequate<br>4 = poor<br>5 = very poor<br>9 = no response |

The responses to questions dealing with these items, when coded from a total of 30 social workers, look as follows:

| Column 1,2 | 3 | 4 | 5 | 6 | Column 1,2 | 3 | 4 | 5 | 6 | Column 1,2 | 3 | 4 | 5 | 6 |
|---|---|---|---|---|---|---|---|---|---|---|---|---|---|---|
| 01 | 1 | 2 | 4 | 3 | 11 | 5 | 1 | 1 | 9 | 21 | 5 | 4 | 2 | 2 |
| 02 | 5 | 4 | 1 | 2 | 12 | 1 | 1 | 1 | 1 | 22 | 5 | 1 | 1 | 1 |
| 03 | 5 | 6 | 2 | 1 | 13 | 1 | 4 | 2 | 4 | 23 | 5 | 2 | 3 | 1 |
| 04 | 5 | 6 | 1 | 5 | 14 | 5 | 1 | 2 | 2 | 24 | 1 | 4 | 1 | 4 |
| 05 | 1 | 3 | 3 | 4 | 15 | 5 | 1 | 1 | 2 | 25 | 5 | 2 | 2 | 1 |
| 06 | 1 | 5 | 2 | 4 | 16 | 5 | 5 | 2 | 3 | 26 | 1 | 6 | 1 | 5 |
| 07 | 5 | 5 | 4 | 5 | 17 | 5 | 2 | 2 | 5 | 27 | 1 | 5 | 1 | 4 |
| 08 | 1 | 4 | 2 | 4 | 18 | 1 | 5 | 3 | 4 | 28 | 5 | 3 | 9 | 2 |
| 09 | 1 | 1 | 1 | 3 | 19 | 1 | 2 | 4 | 1 | 29 | 1 | 1 | 1 | 1 |
| 10 | 1 | 2 | 2 | 2 | 20 | 5 | 5 | 1 | 3 | 30 | 5 | 4 | 2 | 3 |

We shall return to these data in the Practice Sheets, which follow immediately.

# PRACTICE SHEETS

1.  Let us return to the table used at the beginning of this Chapter.

| | Male | | | Female | | | |
|---|---|---|---|---|---|---|---|
| | Single | Married | Total | Single | Married | Total | TOTAL |
| SDSU | 700 | 200 | 900 | 800 | 300 | 1,100 | 2,000 |
| UCSD | 1,000 | 500 | 1,500 | 700 | 300 | 1,000 | 2,500 |
| USD | 500 | 100 | 600 | 600 | 100 | 700 | 1,300 |
| Total | 2,200 | 800 | 3,000 | 2,100 | 700 | 2,800 | 5,800 |

Answer the following questions based upon the information in this table.

a)   What percentage of males at SDSU is single?

b)   What is the ratio of married males to married females at UCSD?

c)   What proportion of the total students in the study is married?

d)   What percentage of the total females in the study is single?

e)   If you were a single male and would like to go to the school with the greatest likelihood of providing you with the companionship of a single female, which school would you go to? Explain your answer.

f)   Conversely, if you were a single female, passionately desirous of relating to single males, which school would you choose? On second thought, don't go anywhere; I am sure we can arrange something right here. But then, again, maybe you had better answer the question anyway — and explain yourself, please.

2.  On a recent test, the 25 students in the Physical Education 347 class (Field Hockey Without a Puck) received the following scores:

86 89 92 88 84 90 86 91 87 89 85 84 87 84 86 88 85 86 87 96 86 88 85 85 87

On the basis of this information, please perform the following odious tasks:

a)   Construct a frequency distribution of these scores; use the raw scores and do not group them into intervals.

b)   Add a column of cumulative frequencies.

c)   Add a column of percentages.

d)   Add a column of cumulative percentages.

e)   What percentile does the student with a score of 90 fall at? What does that mean?

f)   What is the mode of the above distribution?

3.  In a study of psychologists in our area, one question dealt with age at last birthday. The raw data look as follows:

24  26  26  36  46  56  58  47  36  27  27  24  25  28  28  37  49
60  62  49  40  30  32  32  30  25  34  41  34  51  33  68  33  31
31  23  29  35  41  51  35  33  71  25  34  44  52  32  25  29

Now, by a series of brilliant maneuvers, group the data into intervals of your choice; discuss why you made the choice, and interpret the data. Also, for each of your class intervals, calculate the midpoint of the interval.

4.  Using the coded data at the end of this last chapter, please answer the following:

    a)  Tally the number of males and females, and develop a table showing the sex distribution of this group. What is the ratio of males to females?

    b)  Construct a table presenting the data regarding marital status. Does it make sense to collapse some of these categories? Also, include percentages in this table. Interpret the table.

    c)  Construct a table presenting the data for age. Do you want to collapse? Be my guest. Add percentages and interpret.

    d)  Do the same for health, but this time think of how you could trichotomize (divide into 3 categories) or dichotomize (divide into 2 categories) the data, and after you have thought about it, do it. Interpret the data.

5.  Again, using the same data, construct and interpret tables comparing two of the variables, as follows:

    a)  Sex and age.

    b)  Age and health.

    c)  Sex and health.

    d)  Marital status and health.

    e)  Age and marital status.

# CHAPTER 5
# MEASURES OF CENTRAL TENDENCY

Basically, the purpose of so-called "measures of central tendency" is to enable you to describe a population or a set of data in a quick, simple, and easily understandable way. If we look at the current first-year class as the State University School of Social Work, for example, we might ask questions like:

1.    How old are *most* of the students?

2.    What is the marital status of the *"typical"* student?

3.    Which undergraduate college has contributed *more* students to our class than any other undergraduate college?

Obviously, these questions are designed to get at some kind of "central" description of our students. If we respond to these questions by stating, for example, that *most* of the students are between 20 and 25 years of age; or that the marital status of the *typical* student is single; or that *more* students received their BA from HI University than from any other college — then we are obviously presenting a generalized picture of these students. We are certainly not describing all of our students in detail: we know that there are some who are over 25 or even 30 years of age; some who are married; and many who come from undergraduate programs other than HI-U. The goal here, however, is to describe our students in terms of their "central tendency"; other measures will take care of the deviants in the next chapter.

Statistically, we have three basic measures of central tendency: the mode, the median, and the mean (students with a behaviorist orientation might think of these as M & M & M's). We shall now discuss each of these in detail.

## THE MODE
Actually, the mode is a measure which need not even be computed, as it becomes obvious from merely looking at a distribution. The mode, very simply, is usually that value whose frequency is larger than that of all other values in a distribution. It is, in other words, the most frequently appearing value. For example, let us look at the frequency distribution of students' ages that appears at the top of the following page.

Just by looking at this distribution, it is clear that the value 31 years appears with the greatest frequency; i.e., there are 24 31-year olds in this distribution, which is more than there are in any other age category. So, amazingly enough, that is the mode. The mode of the above distribution is 31 years.

A word of caution may be advisable at this time. You probably remember those disgusting second-grade elementary school teachers, who insisted that you must say: "two apples plus three apples equals five apples" and if you dared to just say "five," then the teacher would say, "five what?" and you, like a dummy, had to repeat, "five apples." This bit of learning may stand you in good stead now, because the mode (as well as the median and mean) is always expressed in terms of what it is that we are measuring, so that if you again look at the above distribution, the mode is 31 *years*. The mode is *not* 24!

| Age in Years | Frequency |
|---|---|
| 40 | 1 |
| 39 | 1 |
| 38 | 1 |
| 37 | 3 |
| 36 | 6 |
| 35 | 8 |
| 34 | 12 |
| 33 | 16 |
| 32 | 20 |
| 31 | 24 |
| 30 | 18 |
| 29 | 18 |
| 28 | 12 |
| 27 | 8 |
| 26 | 3 |
| 25 | 2 |
| 24 | 1 |

At times, we get into distributions which are called bimodal; i.e., they really have two high points to them. Thus, for example, the frequency distribution of another class of students may look as follows:

| Age in Years | Frequency |
|---|---|
| 40 | 1 |
| 39 | 3 |
| 38 | 6 |
| 37 | 10 |
| 36 | 18 |
| 35 | 16 |
| 34 | 12 |
| 33 | 6 |
| 32 | 8 |
| 31 | 10 |
| 30 | 15 |
| 29 | 19 |
| 28 | 16 |
| 27 | 13 |
| 26 | 9 |
| 25 | 6 |
| 24 | 2 |

Looking at this distribution, one can see that there are really two points of concentration: the 18 students who are 36 years old, and the 19 students who are 29 years old. Since in such a case we cannot really speak of a single mode, we call this a bi-modal distribution, and the two modes of this distribution are 36 years and 29 years.

When dealing with grouped data (i.e., data that have been arranged in intervals), we have the choice of either determining the modal interval, or using the midpoint of that interval as our mode. For example:

| Age in Years | Frequency |
|---|---|
| 6 — under 8 | 4 |
| 8 — under 10 | 14 |
| 10 — under 12 | 20 |
| 12 — under 14 | 15 |
| 14 — under 16 | 7 |
| Total | 60 |

In this distribution, the age interval that contains more of the population than any other interval is the "10 — under 12" interval, and we can therefore refer to this as our modal interval. We can also determine the midpoint of that modal interval (in this case, 11 years), and call that our mode.

### THE MEDIAN
The median is actually the midpoint of the frequencies of a frequency distribution; i.e., 50 percent of the cases lie above it, and 50 percent of the cases lie below it. Again, it is important to note that the median is not merely the midpoint between the extreme scores. For example, take the following distribution of ages:

| Age in Years | Frequency | Cumulative F |
|---|---|---|
| 1 | 2 | 2 |
| 2 | 2 | 4 |
| 3 | 1 | 5 |
| 4 | 1 | 6 |
| 5 | 5 | 11 |
| Total | 11 | — |

The median here is *not* three years. Rather, the median is four years, because with a total of 11 cases, the median individual (that is, the sixth one) sits within the four-year interval, no matter which way you count. Essentially, if you have ungrouped data or simply an array, you can always find the median by seeing how many values are above and how many values are below a certain value. Again, looking at years, if the array is 3, 4, 5, 5, 7, 8, 9, 9, 10, 12, 13, then our median is 8 years because 5 values are below 8 years, and 5 values are above 8. This simple system always holds true when you have an odd number of observations (a total of 11 in this case). If we have an even number of observations, the median is usually assumed to be half way between the two middle observations. For example, if our observations are 4, 6, 10, and 15, then the median lies between 6 and 10. The average or midpoint between these two numbers is 8, and we could therefore call the median of this distribution 8.

## Computation Of Median For Grouped Data

When we have grouped data (as we usually do) and we are dealing with intervals, the computation of the median becomes a little more difficult. For example:

| Age in Years | Frequency | Cumulative F |
|---|---|---|
| 6 — under 8 | 4 | 4 |
| 8 — under 10 | 14 | 18 |
| 10 — under 12 | 20 | 38 |
| 12 — under 14 | 15 | 53 |
| 14 — under 16 | 7 | 60 |
| Total | 60 | — |

Actually, one way of looking at it is to say that we are trying to find where the 30th child is located. If you want to be more exact, you could say that we want to know where the 30th child ends and the 31st child starts. If we start counting from the top, we get 4 + 14 = 18; but then 18 + 20 = 38, which is too much. So we know that the 30th child must be in that 10 to 12-year category. But where in the 10 to under 12-year category? Is the median 10.2 years or 11 years or 11.9 years? It sometimes helps to visualize the intervals as sections of a log, and these children are sitting spaced out (they're very young children) along this log, and we want to know where the 30th child sits. How far inside the 10 to under 12-year interval does he sit? Well, from a logical viewpoint, we could say that we have accounted for 18 children in the first two categories. That leaves us 12 children to reach our goal of 30; i.e., 12 out of the 20 in that particular interval. Assuming that these kids are sitting spaced equally within the 10 to under 12-year category, we could then say that the 30th child must be $\frac{12}{20}$ of the way into the 2-year interval of 10 to under 12 years. If we say this mathematically, we would say that this child $= \frac{12}{20} \times 2 = 1.2$. In other words, the child is 1.2 years into that 10 to under 12-year interval; he is thus 10 + 1.2 years, or 11.2 years old. Therefore, the median of that distribution is 11.2 years.

The purpose of the above explanation was to help you understand the logic of it all. Usually, of course, we do not go through this kind of an elaborate reasoning process to compute the median of a distribution; we use a formula instead. But please note that the formula is exactly a summary of what we have just done. The formula for the median is:

$$ Md = L_{md} + \left[ \frac{\frac{N}{2} - CF_{bmd}}{f_{md}} \right] W $$

In this formula, $L_{md}$ is the lower limit of the interval which contains the median; N, as usual, is the total number of cases or observations; $CF_{bmd}$ is the sum of the frequencies (the cumulative frequency) up to but not including the interval that contains the median (i.e., before the median interval);

$f_{md}$ is the frequency of the interval that contains the median; and W is the width of the class interval that contains the median. If we now plug in the appropriate numbers for the distribution above, we get:

$$\text{median (Md)} = 10 + \left[ \frac{\frac{60}{2} - 18}{20} \right] 2$$

$$= 10 + \left[ \frac{30 - 18}{20} \right] 2$$

$$= 10 + \left[ \frac{12}{20} \right] \times 2$$

$$= 11.2 \text{ years}$$

Please note again that this is really exactly what we did originally, and all that this formula does is to compress the logic and state it in mathematical terms.

The exact same procedure can, of course, be followed with larger and more complicated frequency distributions. It should also be noted that the median can be used when we have an open-ended interval (for example, 25 years and over), or when the intervals themselves are not equally wide. For example:

### MONTHLY ILLICIT INCOME OF STUDENTS AT USU
### 1979 (approx.)

| Income | Frequency | Cumulative Frequency |
|---|---|---|
| $   0 – 10 | 145 | 145 |
| 11 – 50 | 875 | 1,020 |
| 51 – 75 | 810 | 1,830 |
| 76 – 100 | 1,025 | 2,855 |
| 101 – 125 | 2,130 | 4,985 |
| 126 – 150 | 3,275 | 8,260 |
| 151 – 175 | 3,460 | 11,720 |
| 176 – 200 | 1,315 | 13,035 |
| 201 – 225 | 760 | 13,795 |
| 226 – 250 | 680 | 14,475 |
| 251 – 300 | 525 | 15,000 |
| 301 & over | 360 | 15,360 |
| Total | 15,360 | — |

$$Md = L_{md} + \left[ \frac{\frac{N}{2} - CF_{bmd}}{f_{md}} \right] W$$

Again, we are looking for the "middle value" in this distribution of 15,360 incomes. Obviously, that middle value is in the interval that corresponds to the frequency of $\frac{15,360}{2} = 7,680$. Looking at our cumulative frequency, we can see that we had accounted for 4,985 cases up to and including the $101-125 interval, but the next interval ($126-150) brings us beyond the desired frequency of 7,680. We know, therefore, that our median interval is the $126-150 interval, and that our median is hiding somewhere therein. Looking now at our formula, we know that $L_{md} = 126$ (i.e., the lower limit of the interval which contains the median). Furthermore, we have already calculated $\frac{N}{2} = 7,680$. The cumulative frequency up to, but not including our median interval ($CF_{bmd}$) is equal to 4,985; the frequency of the median interval ($f_{md}$) is 3,275; and the width of that median interval is 25. Substituting all this into our formula, we get:

$$Md = 126 + \left[\frac{7680-4985}{3275}\right] \; 25$$

$$= 126 + \left[\frac{2695}{3275}\right] 25$$

$$= 126 + \;\; (.823) \;\; 25$$

$$= 126 + \;\; 20.58$$

$$= \$146.58$$

Our median, then, = $146.58. Please note that in the above example we are dealing with unequal intervals in the distribution, ranging from an interval of $10 ($0-10), to several intervals of $25 ($101-125, $126-150, etc.), to one interval of $40 ($11-50), one interval of $50 ($251-300), and one interval of indeterminate extent ($301 and over). In spite of this confusing mishmash of intervals, and in spite of the fact that we have that open-ended interval which extends to God-knows-where, we are able to calculate the median, and the value we obtained is indeed the monthly illicit income of that middle (or median) student, with 50 percent of the incomes above that value, and 50 percent of the incomes below that value.

## THE MEAN
The mean is the measure of central tendency with which students are usually most familiar. It is commonly known as the "average," and if you remember the days of worrying about your average in elementary school, you'll remember taking all the grades you received on the tests and dividing the sum by the number of tests you had received. That "average" was the mean. For example, if your grades on 6 tests had been 90, 100, 90, 90, 100, and 80, and you wanted to know what your average was, you would have first added these:

$$\begin{array}{r} 90 \\ 100 \\ 90 \\ 90 \\ 100 \\ \underline{80} \\ 550 \end{array}$$

Secondly, you would have divided by the number of tests you had:

$$\frac{91.67}{6 \overline{)550.00}}$$

Your average (or mean) was 91.67. Note that you were able to arrive at the mean here without even constructing a frequency distribution. If you were a little bit more sophisticated, or if there were 20 quizzes instead of only 6, you might even have moved to writing things down as a frequency distribution as follows:

| Grade (x) | Frequency (f) | fx |
|---|---|---|
| 80 | 1 | 80 |
| 90 | 3 | 270 |
| 100 | 2 | 200 |
| **Total** | **6** | **550** |

You then again divide 550 by 6 and get your same average of 91.67. Basically, then, the mean is the sum of the values times their frequencies, divided by the number of observations. The formula is:

$$\text{Mean} = \frac{\Sigma fx}{N}$$

In this formula, x stands for the values, f for frequencies, that funny $\Sigma$ is the Greek letter Sigma and means "sum of," and N is again the number of observations.

Obviously, things get much more complicated when we deal with class intervals and with a larger number of values. It then becomes necessary to construct a frequency distribution, and it is advisable to use two short cuts in the calculations. First, choose a "guessed mean" and call it 0; and second, assign the intervals a value of plus or minus 1 for each interval of deviance from the guessed mean (don't drop the book yet — it really becomes quite simple soon). For example, let us look at an age distribution of individuals residing in a given area.

| Age in Years (x) | Frequency (f) |
|---|---|
| 0 — 9 | 40 |
| 10 — 19 | 30 |
| 20 — 29 | 22 |
| 30 — 39 | 25 |
| 40 — 49 | 22 |
| 50 — 59 | 18 |
| 60 — 69 | 13 |
| 70 — 79 | 7 |
| 80 — 89 | 2 |
| 90 — 99 | 1 |
| **Total** | **180** |

Trying to calculate the mean of this distribution the way we "averaged" your grades would involve some horrendous numbers — just imagine multiplying the midpoints of each interval (5, 15, 25, 35, etc.) by the frequencies (40, 30, 22, etc.), adding it all up and then dividing by 180 — TOO MUCH!

So let us try the short cuts: First, let us guess at a mean — perhaps it is somewhere in the 30-39 year interval. We will therefore call that interval "0"; actually, we are calling the midpoint of the interval "0"; or, if you like, we can say that we are subtracting 35 years from all the scores. Secondly, since we are dealing with equal intervals, let us call each 10-unit interval "1." Our table now has a new column and looks as follows:

| Age in Years (x) | Frequency (f) | Coded Midpoint (d) |
|---|---|---|
| 0 — 9 | 40 | –3 |
| 10 — 19 | 30 | –2 |
| 20 — 29 | 22 | –1 |
| 30 — 39 | 25 | 0 |
| 40 — 49 | 22 | 1 |
| 50 — 59 | 18 | 2 |
| 60 — 69 | 13 | 3 |
| 70 — 79 | 7 | 4 |
| 80 — 89 | 2 | 5 |
| 90 — 99 | 1 | 6 |
| Total | 180 | |

To repeat: what we have done is to guess that the mean will be somewhere in the 30 to 39 year interval, and have, therefore, assigned this interval a coded number 0. By the way, you need not fear "guessing" wrong; it will work out even if your guess is a poor one. If the 30 to 39 year interval = 0 and if we are going to let 10 years equal one, we can then assign coded values of –1 to the 20 to 29 year interval, –2 to the 10 to 19 year interval, and –3 to the 0 to 9 year interval. Similarly, we can assign values of +1 to the 40 to 49 year interval, +2 to the 50 to 59 year interval, etc. Please note that we have done two things:

1) We have called the midpoint of the 30 to 39 year interval 0, and,

2) we have called every 10 year interval 1.

This is like cheating, and we will have to put it all back in the end; but in the meantime we will be able to deal with much smaller numbers.

The next step is to multiply each frequency by the coded midpoint and enter this in the column labeled "fd."

| Age in Years (x) | Frequency (f) | Coded Midpoint (d) | fd |
|---|---|---|---|
| 0 – 9 | 40 | −3 | −120 |
| 10 – 19 | 30 | −2 | −60 |
| 20 – 29 | 22 | −1 | −22 |
| 30 – 39 | 25 | 0 | 0 |
| 40 – 49 | 22 | 1 | 22 |
| 50 – 59 | 18 | 2 | 36 |
| 60 – 69 | 13 | 3 | 39 |
| 70 – 79 | 7 | 4 | 28 |
| 80 – 89 | 2 | 5 | 10 |
| 90 – 99 | 1 | 6 | 6 |
| Total | 180 | | $\Sigma fd = -61$ |

We then add this column to arrive at $\Sigma fd = -61$. In order to get our mean, we divide this sum by N:

$$\frac{\Sigma fd}{N} = \frac{-61}{180} = -.338$$

Now we have to put back what we took away. First of all, we had called each 10 year interval 1, and we therefore now have to multiply −.338 by 10 which equals −3.38. Furthermore, we have to give back the 35 that we stole by calling the 30 to 39 year interval 0. Then, 35 − 3.38 = 31.62, and that is our mean!

Now that you hopefully understand what we did and why we did it, we can give you a rather simple formula:

$$\text{Mean} = X_o + \frac{(\Sigma fd)}{N} \ W$$

In this formula, $X_o$ stands for our "guessed" mean or the midpoint of the interval of our "guessed" mean; d stands for the coded "deviations" from the guessed mean; and the other symbols mean what they usually mean.

Plugging in the appropriate numbers for the above problem, we get:

$$\text{Mean} = 35 + \frac{(-61)}{180} \ 10$$

$$= 35 + (-.338) \ 10$$

$$= 35 - 3.38$$

$$= 31.62$$

Let's try one other example. Suppose we are interested in determining the mean number of units of undergraduate social science courses taken by current social work students. Our frequency distribution looks as follows:

| Number of Units (x) | Frequency (f) |
|---|---|
| 0 – 3 | 2 |
| 4 – 7 | 4 |
| 8 – 11 | 3 |
| 12 – 15 | 12 |
| 16 – 19 | 18 |
| 20 – 23 | 26 |
| 24 – 27 | 35 |
| 28 – 31 | 34 |
| 32 – 35 | 12 |
| 36 – 39 | 23 |
| 40 – 43 | 0 |
| 44 – 47 | 1 |
| **Total** | **170** |

If we now proceed as previously outlined, we will guess at our mean and label the midpoint of that interval "0"; also, we will call each interval one. Just to illustrate that you don't even have to be a good guesser, let's purposely guess way out, and call the 12 to 15 unit interval "0." Our new table, complete with coded midpoints and "fd," then looks as follows:

| Number of Units (x) | Frequency (f) | Coded Midpoint (d) | fd |
|---|---|---|---|
| 0 – 3 | 2 | –3 | –6 |
| 4 – 7 | 4 | –2 | –8 |
| 8 – 11 | 3 | –1 | –3 |
| 12 – 15 | 12 | 0 | 0 |
| 16 – 19 | 18 | 1 | 18 |
| 20 – 23 | 26 | 2 | 52 |
| 24 – 27 | 35 | 3 | 105 |
| 28 – 31 | 34 | 4 | 136 |
| 32 – 35 | 12 | 5 | 60 |
| 36 – 39 | 23 | 6 | 138 |
| 40 – 43 | 0 | 7 | 0 |
| 44 – 47 | 1 | 8 | 8 |
| **Total** | **170** | | $\Sigma fd = 500$ |

$$\text{Mean} = X_o + \frac{(\Sigma\ fd)}{N}\ W$$

$$= 13.5 + \left(\frac{500}{170}\right) 4$$

$$= 13.5 + (2.95)\ \ 4$$

$$= 13.5 + 11.8$$

$$= 25.3\ \text{units}$$

We conclude, then, that the mean number of units in social sciences, taken by current social work students, was 25.3 units.

## USE OF MODE, MEDIAN AND MEAN

In attempting to describe the central tendency or the general characteristics of a population, the question arises as to which of the measures of central tendency one should use. Regrettably, there is no single answer. It depends upon what the distribution is like, and what it is that you are trying to point out. The mode, for example, is the most useful tool for very quickly determining where most cases fall, and can be ascertained merely by inspection. The median is most useful when we have a rather skewed or lopsided distribution and/or when there is an open-ended interval. The mean is the most sophisticated measure of central tendency and is most useful for further computations; but it cannot be used with open-ended intervals, and has the disadvantage of being very sensitive to extremes. For example, let us go back to some exam grades that a student might have received in elementary school. Let us say that his first 6 grades were as follows: 100, 90, 90, 90, 100, and 100. If we average these grades (i.e., get the mean) we find that the mean is equal to 570 divided by 6, which, equals 95. But then a tragedy takes place: either the student didn't study or his seat was changed, for on the next exam he gets a 30. If we average the seven grades including the 30, we find that his mean grade is 600 divided by 7 which equals 85.7. Please note that one poor grade (i.e., one extreme score) lowered his average by almost 10 points. As we have said before, the mean is highly sensitive to extremes.

As an illustration of the application of measures of central tendency, let us take the annual income of 40 employees in a factory. Their incomes are: 5 at $5,000, 20 at $7,000, 10 at $10,000, 2 at $25,000, 2 at $40,000, and 1 at $100,000. Which measure of central tendency is most indicative of the income of these workers? The mode is $7,000 (20 workers earn that much per year). The median is also $7,000. The mean, however, is $12,375. Undoubtedly, in a battle between union and management, the union would stress the median income to indicate that workers are being underpaid. Management, on the other hand, would stress the mean to indicate that the "average" worker is making $12,375 per year. Both are correct and it merely becomes a question of what it is that one is trying to prove.

If a distribution is perfectly symmetrical, then, of course, the mean and median will be the same. In a unimodal distribution, the mode in a symmetrical distribution will also be at the same value, but this is not true in the case of a bimodal distribution.

# PRACTICE SHEETS

1. The following three frequency distributions show the distribution of children by age in years.

| Age | Group A | Group B | Group C |
|---|---|---|---|
| 5 | 7 | 2 | 4 |
| 6 | 8 | 3 | 8 |
| 7 | 10 | 30 | 16 |
| 8 | 6 | 4 | 8 |
| 9 | 9 | 1 | 4 |
| Total | 40 | 40 | 40 |

a) Compute the mean for each group.
b) Compute the median for each group.
c) Compute the mode for each group.

2. The following are also distributions of ages of children:

| | Group A | Group B | Group C | Group D |
|---|---|---|---|---|
| 6 and under 8 | 11 | 4 | 50 | 20 |
| 8 and under 10 | 12 | 14 | 4 | 30 |
| 10 and under 12 | 17 | 20 | 5 | 10 |
| 12 and under 14 | 11 | 15 | 1 | 0 |
| 14 and under 16 | 9 | 7 | 0 | 0 |
| Total | 60 | 60 | 60 | 60 |

a) Compute the mean for each group.
b) Compute the median for each group.
c) Compute the mode for each group.

3. The following is the percentage distribution of a sample of Public Assistance Cases by type of case and monthly income:

| | | Type of Case | |
|---|---|---|---|
| | Total cases | One-person cases | Family cases |
| | Percentage distribution | | |
| Under $ 50 | 10.5 | 25.9 | 2.1 |
| $ 50 – 99 | 45.6 | 63.2 | 11.1 |
| 100 – 149 | 18.8 | 8.8 | 33.8 |
| 150 – 199 | 12.3 | 0.9 | 25.8 |
| 200 – 249 | 5.7 | 0.7 | 11.6 |
| 250 – 299 | 3.0 | 0.5 | 7.1 |
| 300 and over | 4.1 | – | 8.5 |
| Total | 100.0 | 100.0 | 100.0 |

For those categories of cases for which it makes sense (Total, One-person, Family cases), calculate:

a)    the means

b)    the medians

c)    the modes

4.    For the following, respond by answering mean, median, or mode; multiple responses as possible.

    a)    The number of cases above this statistic is always the same as the number of cases below it.

    b)    The value of this statistic is usually not greatly affected by the addition of one or two more cases.

    c)    The value of this statistic may be greatly affected by the addition of any new values.

    d)    In a symmetrical distribution, this statistic will always fall at the point of symmetry.

5.    The mean annual family income of the residents of Husiatyn is reported to be $8,465; the median family income is reported to be only $4,526. How is this possible? Please explain. Also, pray tell, which of these two statistics best represents the "typical" family income of the residents of Husiatyn?

6.    The table below indicates the population and percentage distribution of U.S. residents by age for the years 1940, 1960, and 1976. For each of these years, calculate mean, median, mode. Discuss differences among the statistics within and between the years.

| Age | Population in Millions | | | Percentage Dist. | | |
|---|---|---|---|---|---|---|
| | 1940 | 1960 | 1976 | 1940 | 1960 | 1976 |
| 0 – 9 | 21.2 | 39.0 | 32.6 | 16.1 | 21.7 | 15.2 |
| 10 – 19 | 24.0 | 30.0 | 41.0 | 18.3 | 17.0 | 19.1 |
| 20 – 29 | 22.7 | 21.7 | 37.1 | 17.2 | 12.1 | 17.3 |
| 30 – 39 | 19.7 | 24.4 | 26.1 | 15.0 | 13.7 | 12.1 |
| 40 – 49 | 17.1 | 22.5 | 22.8 | 13.0 | 12.6 | 10.6 |
| 50 – 59 | 13.2 | 18.0 | 22.8 | 10.0 | 10.0 | 10.6 |
| 60 – 69 | 8.6 | 13.4 | 17.6 | 6.4 | 7.4 | 8.2 |
| 70 – 79 | 4.0 | 7.9 | 10.8 | 3.0 | 4.3 | 5.1 |
| 80 – 89 | 1.0 | 2.0 | 3.2 | .8 | 1.0 | 1.5 |
| 90 – 99 | .2 | .5 | .6 | .2 | .2 | .3 |
| Totals | 131.7 | 179.4 | 214.6 | 100.0 | 100.0 | 100.0 |

# CHAPTER 6
# MEASURES OF DISPERSION

The measures of central tendency give us some notion of the "typical" values of the frequency distribution. Measures of dispersion, on the other hand, tell us how spread out the frequency distribution is, or how many individuals really deviate from the norm, and how much they deviate.

## THE RANGE

This one is by far the easiest of all so-called "measures of dispersion." If I ask you to tell me about the ages of your closest friends, you might say that most of them are about 25 years old (that's the mode, you remember), and that they *range* in age from 22 years to 35 years; and that is all there is to that. The range of your friends' ages, then, is 22 to 35 years; or we might say that their ages cover a range of 13 years (35 – 22 = 13). The range, then, is the distance from the smallest value of the variable to the largest value of the variable.

Obviously, the range is a very crude measure of dispersion. In the above example, for all we know, the vast majority of your friends may be between 22 and 26 years, and only one poor soul is 35 years old; or, it may be the other way around. The range, therefore, gives us only a very cursory notion of a distribution; but then, again, it gives it to us with no difficulties whatsoever. This leads, of course, to the philosophical question of whether anything that we get so easily is really worth very much—but we won't delve into that sphere of speculation at this point in time.

## THE VARIANCE AND STANDARD DEVIATION

If we have a class of students in which everyone is 10 years old, then obviously we have no deviation. If, on the other hand, we have a class of students in which some are 6 years old, some 7 years old, several are 10 years old, and a few are 13 and 14 years old, we may have a class in which the mean age is 10 years, but in which there is a considerable amount of deviation from this mean. Such deviation is usually called variability. In other words, with measures of dispersion, we are interested in the extent to which the cases in a frequency distribution vary from each other. Frequently, variability is defined as the opposite of clustering. In other words, if most of the data cluster around one value (everybody is 10 years old) then obviously we have very little or no variability. If, on the other hand, the ages within the group are spread out over a number of years, then we obviously have considerable variability in the group (i.e., very little clustering).

This notion may be further illustrated by the use of some histograms. (No, this has nothing to do with sterilization procedures for grammies; histograms are relatives of bar-graphs). Looking at three different groups of students, we might find the following distributions:

| Age | Group A | Group B | Group C |
|---|---|---|---|
| 8 | 0 | 7 | 4 |
| 9 | 2 | 7 | 8 |
| 10 | 30 | 8 | 16 |
| 11 | 4 | 8 | 8 |
| 12 | 2 | 7 | 4 |
| 13 | 2 | 3 | 0 |
| Total | 40 | 40 | 40 |

Presenting these distributions in the form of histograms would lead to the following:

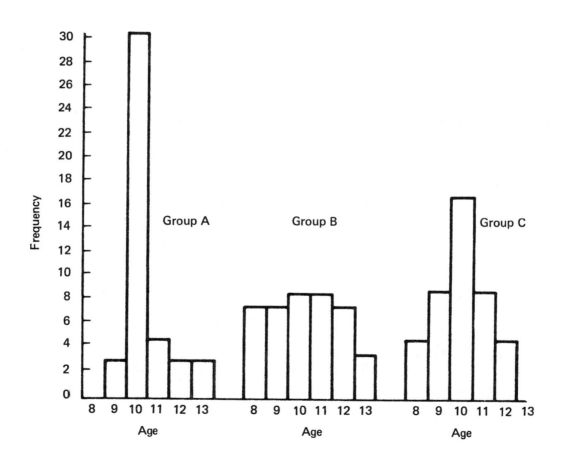

Looking at these histograms, it should become immediately obvious to anyone (or almost anyone) that there is a great concentration of 10 year olds in Group A—30 out of the 40 children are 10 years old. We would therefore say that there is very much clustering in that group — and consequently, very little variability (i.e., the students in that group vary very little). In Group B, on the other hand, we have almost no clustering at all — almost the same number of children are 8, 9, 10, 11, and 12 years old. Consequently, we would say that there is almost no clustering in that group, and its variability must be considerable (verily I say unto you, these students vary very vastly). In our third group, Group C, we see some concentration or clustering, but certainly not as much as had been found in Group A. In terms of variability, then, Group B has the greatest variability, followed by Group C, with Group A having the least variability.

As some of you have undoubtedly surmised by now, there must be some mathematical way of measuring the variability of a distribution. The most useful and most common measure of variability measures the extent to which the values in a frequency distribution vary *from the mean.* Let us take the following frequency distribution as an example:

| Age | f |
|---|---|
| 7 | 5 |
| 8 | 7 |
| 9 | 16 |
| 10 | 7 |
| 11 | 5 |
| Total | 40 |

If we calculate the mean of this group, we will find that it is 9 years. We now want to determine the amount of variability that exists in this group; i.e., how much deviation exists from that mean of 9 years? Obviously, we will call nine years "0," since that is our mean and the 16 children who are 9 years old do not deviate from the mean at all. Eight years is then a deviation of −1, 7 years a deviation of −2, etc. In the form of a table, this looks as follows:

| Age | f | d |
|---|---|---|
| 7 | 5 | −2 |
| 8 | 7 | −1 |
| 9 | 16 | 0 |
| 10 | 7 | 1 |
| 11 | 5 | 2 |
| Total | 40 | |

To give each deviation its proper weight, we should multiply the deviation by the frequency, resulting in a new column called fd, which would look as follows:

| fd |
|---|
| −10 |
| −7 |
| 0 |
| 7 |
| 10 |
| Total 0 |

50

If we now add this column, we end up with 0, and of course we must end up with 0, because the mean is our balancing point, and the positive and negative deviations on each side of it will always balance each other out. We are thus at a dead end. But wait, there is hope yet: we can get around this impasse by getting rid of the minus signs, and the way in which we do that is to square each deviation (remember — a negative number multiplied by another negative number yields a positive number). We will then multiply the *squared* deviation by its frequency. Our table now looks as follows:

| Age | f | d | $d^2$ | $fd^2$ |
|---|---|---|---|---|
| 7 | 5 | −2 | 4 | 20 |
| 8 | 7 | −1 | 1 | 7 |
| 9 | 16 | 0 | 0 | 0 |
| 10 | 7 | 1 | 1 | 7 |
| 11 | 5 | 2 | 4 | 20 |
| Totals | 40 | | | $\Sigma fd^2 = 54$ |

What we now have is that $\Sigma fd^2$ is the sum of (the frequencies) times (the squared deviations). But just as with the mean, we are really after a sort of "average deviation," and therefore we have to divide 54 by N:

$$54 \div 40 = 1.35$$

This indeed is a measure of variability, called the variance, or $s^2$. A considerable number of advanced statistical procedures make use of the variance. But for the present time, we can arrive at an even more useful measure of deviation when we remember that we cheated: we squared those deviations in order to get rid of the minus signs, and what we now have to do, in all fairness, is to take the square root of 1.35, which turns out to be approximately 1.16. This means that the "average deviation," usually called the standard deviation (or s), is 1.16 years for this particular distribution.

Once again, we have gone through a rather tortuous process to explain what the standard deviation really is, and how one can arrive at it logically. As in the case of the mean, there is a somewhat simple computational formula for the standard deviation for simple ungrouped data, which is:

$$s = \sqrt{\frac{\Sigma fd^2}{N}}$$

Actually, when dealing with samples rather than with entire populations, we use a slightly different formula in order to obtain a better estimate of the standard deviation. The reasons for this lie in a realm of mathematics far beyond me or thee; so just take my word for it. For samples we simply change the formula to:

$$s = \sqrt{\frac{\Sigma fd^2}{n - 1}}$$

Things again become slightly different when we deal with data which have been grouped in intervals. For example, let us return to the table used for computing the mean, and repeat it again:

| Age in Years (x) | Frequency (f) | Coded Midpoint (d) | fd |
|---|---|---|---|
| 0 – 9 | 40 | –3 | –120 |
| 10 – 19 | 30 | –2 | –60 |
| 20 – 29 | 22 | –1 | –22 |
| 30 – 39 | 25 | 0 | 0 |
| 40 – 49 | 22 | 1 | 22 |
| 50 – 59 | 18 | 2 | 36 |
| 60 – 69 | 13 | 3 | 39 |
| 70 – 79 | 7 | 4 | 28 |
| 80 – 89 | 2 | 5 | 10 |
| 90 – 99 | 1 | 6 | 6 |
| Total | 180 | | $\Sigma fd = -61$ |

If we now add our two new columns ($d^2$ and $fd^2$) on to it, we get the following:

| Age in Years (x) | Frequency (f) | Coded Midpoint (d) | fd | $d^2$ | $fd^2$ |
|---|---|---|---|---|---|
| 0 – 9 | 40 | –3 | –120 | 9 | 360 |
| 10 – 19 | 30 | –2 | –60 | 4 | 120 |
| 20 – 29 | 22 | –1 | –22 | 1 | 22 |
| 30 – 39 | 25 | 0 | 0 | 0 | 0 |
| 40 – 49 | 22 | 1 | 22 | 1 | 22 |
| 50 – 59 | 18 | 2 | 36 | 4 | 72 |
| 60 – 69 | 13 | 3 | 39 | 9 | 117 |
| 70 – 79 | 7 | 4 | 28 | 16 | 112 |
| 80 – 89 | 2 | 5 | 10 | 25 | 50 |
| 90 – 99 | 1 | 6 | 6 | 36 | 36 |
| Total | 180 | | $\Sigma fd = -61$ | | $\Sigma fd^2 = 911$ |

Once the table is set up this way, we can calculate the mean and the standard deviation in one continuous procedure. We have already calculated the mean in the previous chapter by saying:

$$\text{mean} = X_o + \left( \frac{\Sigma fd}{N} \right) W = 31.62 \text{ years}$$

But, in assigning our 0-point to the 30 to 40 year interval, we had established a "guessed" mean of 35 years, and our columns of fd and $fd^2$ are based upon that guess. In order to account for the fact that this guess was slightly off (although quite close), we will have to include some "correction" in our calculations of the standard deviation. Remember, please, that the standard deviation is measured in terms of deviation *from the mean.*

The formula for the standard deviation now, including the "correction," is:

$$\text{std. dev.} = W\sqrt{\frac{\Sigma\, fd^2}{N} - \left(\frac{\Sigma\, fd}{N}\right)^2}$$

If we now substitute the appropriate numbers for the symbols, we get:

$$s = 10\sqrt{\frac{911}{180} - \left(\frac{-61}{180}\right)^2}$$

$$= 10\sqrt{\frac{911}{180} - \frac{3721}{32400}}$$

$$= 10\sqrt{5.061 - .114}$$

$$= 10\sqrt{4.947}$$

$$= 10 \times 2.22$$

$$= 22.2 \text{ years}$$

What we have, then, is a distribution with a mean of 31.62 years, and a standard deviation of 22.2 years.

What the above indicates is that when you have a rather simple distribution, or the mean is a whole number (like 12, or 37), you can use the simple formula for the standard deviation. When, however, you are dealing with a more complex distribution, and/or when the mean is not a whole number, and when you had to "guess" at the mean, you must use the more complex formula in order to correct any errors you made in your guess. This also frees you from having to feel that you must guess correctly; the formula will automatically correct your mistakes. Let us look at one other distribution, where we will purposely make a poor guess at the mean, and see what happens:

### Age Distribution Of Students At University Of Dubova (1902)

| Age in Years | f | d | fd | $d^2$ | $fd^2$ |
|---|---|---|---|---|---|
| 15 — 19 | 20 | -2 | -40 | 4 | 80 |
| 20 — 24 | 40 | -1 | -40 | 1 | 40 |
| 25 — 29 | 20 | 0 | 0 | 0 | 0 |
| 30 — 34 | 20 | 1 | 20 | 1 | 20 |
| 35 — 39 | 40 | 2 | 80 | 4 | 160 |
| 40 — 44 | 30 | 3 | 90 | 9 | 270 |
| 45 — 49 | 30 | 4 | 120 | 16 | 480 |
| Totals | 200 | | $\Sigma fd = 230$ | | $\Sigma fd^2 = 1{,}050$ |

$$\text{Mean} = X_0 + \left(\frac{\Sigma fd}{N}\right) W$$

$$= 27.5 + \left(\frac{230}{200}\right) 5$$

$$= 27.5 + 5.75$$

$$= 33.25 \text{ years}$$

$$s = W\sqrt{\frac{\Sigma fd^2}{N} - \left(\frac{\Sigma fd}{N}\right)^2}$$

$$= 5\sqrt{\frac{1050}{200} - \left(\frac{230}{200}\right)^2}$$

$$= 5\sqrt{5.25 - \frac{52,900}{40,000}}$$

$$= 5\sqrt{5.25 - 1.32}$$

$$= 5\sqrt{3.93}$$

$$= 5 \times 1.98$$

$$= 9.9 \text{ years}$$

We can see here that our "poor guess" really made no difference, because it was corrected in the formula (that's that – 1.32).

Once again, for samples we have to use n–1 in the formula. Thus, the formula for the standard deviation of a sample is:

$$s = W\sqrt{\frac{\Sigma fd^2}{n-1} - \left(\frac{\Sigma fd}{n-1}\right)^2}$$

An appropriate question at this point in time, or at any point in time, for that matter, might be: "So what? What does it all mean?" What does a standard deviation of 3.6 or 1.5 or 17.8 mean? Well, first of all, it should be noted that the standard deviation is not an abstract number, but like the mean, median, and mode, is always in the same units as the original variable was. In other words, if we have been measuring years, then our standard deviation will be in years – 3.6 years, or 1.5 years, or 17.8 years. Secondly, on a rather intuitive basis, we can say that the standard deviation is sort of the "average amount of deviation" in a distribution, and thus gives us some notion of how concentrated or how spread out a distribution is. Thus, a distribution with a standard deviation of 17.8 years has much greater variability than a distribution with a standard deviation of only 3.6 or 1.5 years. Furthermore, the standard deviation operates mathematically in such a way, that in *any* frequency distribution, *at least 75 percent of the cases* are within the range of plus or minus two standard deviations from the mean. What this means is that if, for example, we have a population with a mean age of 15 years and a standard deviation of 2 years, then at least 75 percent of all cases must fall between 11 years (15 – 4) and 19 years (15 + 4).

Finally, the standard deviation will become much more meaningful to you when we apply it to several other concepts, which will be dealt with post haste in the chapters to come.

## PRACTICE SHEET

1. Take the data presented in Question 1 of Chapter 5. Without any calculations, which of the three groups, do you think, has the greatest variability? Why? Which group has the least variability? Why? Now calculate the standard deviation for Group C.

2. For the data presented in Question 2 for Chapter 5, what is the range of each of these groups? What are their standard deviations?

3. The following is a distribution of ages. (Note: the midpoints of the intervals are 18.5, 23.5, 28.5, etc. Why?)

| Age | f | |
|---|---|---|
| 16 – 20 | 2 | |
| 21 – 25 | 1 | |
| 26 – 30 | 5 | |
| 31 – 35 | 11 | |
| 36 – 40 | 12 | |
| 41 – 45 | 16 | |
| 46 – 50 | 8 | |
| 51 – 55 | 16 | |
| 56 – 60 | 7 | |
| 61 – 65 | 3 | |
| 66 – 70 | 2 | |
| 71 – 75 | 1 | |
| 76 – 80 | 10 | |
| 81 – 85 | 3 | |
| 86 – 90 | 3 | |
| **Total** | **100** | |

Use the space in the table above to fill in any additional columns you might need to calculate:

a)  the mean

b)  the standard deviation (assume that this is a population)

c)  the median

d)  the mode

e)  the range

f)  interpret your findings, paying special attention to any differences you might find between the mean, median, and mode

g)  re-calculate the standard deviation, assuming this to be a sample.

4. Do the same for the data from Chapter 5, Question 6.

# CHAPTER 7
# THE NORMAL DISTRIBUTION

I hope that by this time you have learned that populations come in all shapes and sizes as far as their frequency distributions are concerned. There are flattened out ones (much variability) and thin, high ones (little variability); they may be nice and symmetrical, or they may be badly skewed (that's a sort of drunk distribution). Some examples of different distributions are beautifully illustrated below.

**Age Distribution Of U.S. Population (1960)**
(a skewed distribution with considerable variability)

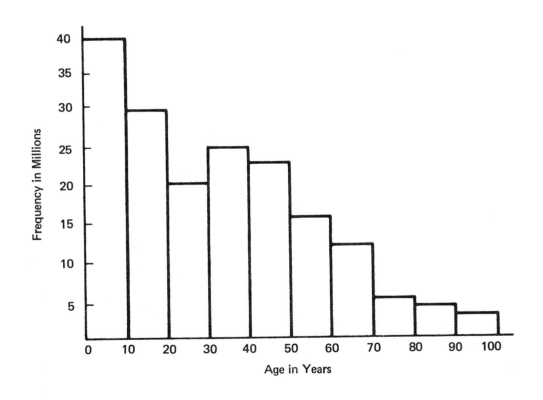

## Age Of Entering College Freshmen
### (skewed, with little variability)

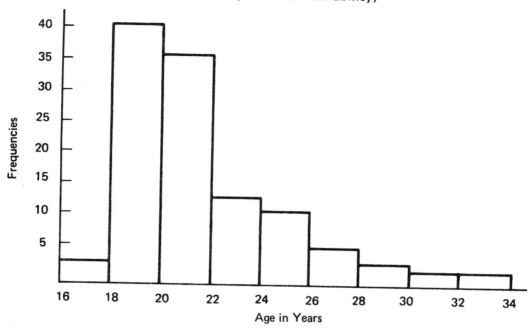

Age in Years

## Height Distribution Of 300 Male Students at OXU
### (fairly symmetrical; with frequency polygon superimposed)

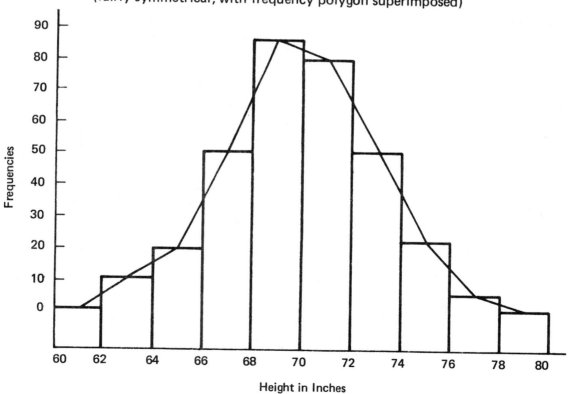

Height in Inches

In this last distribution, I slipped in the phrase "with frequency polygon superimposed." All that this means is that in addition to presenting data in the form of a histogram, we can present data graphically by joining the midpoints of the tops of the bars, and thus end up with what used to be called a line graph. But you are adults now, so we are going to call it a "frequency polygon." In fact, we rather like frequency polygons — they are easier to draw, especially when you get to rounding them out more, which is always fun. If we round out our frequency polygon for the height distribution of 300 male students at OXU, it looks approximately as follows:

**Frequency Polygon For Heights Of 300 Male Students At OXU**

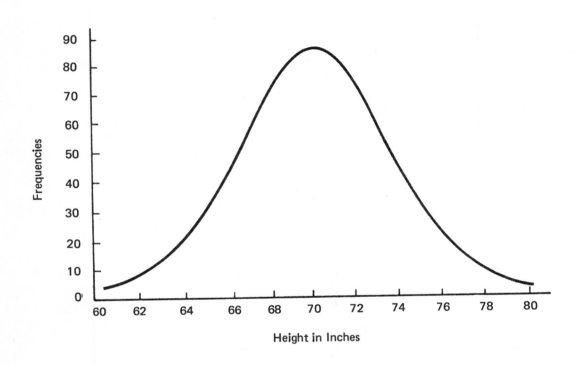

This now begins to look like the distribution that students are so fond of — that star of all distributions — *the normal distribution.* Regrettably, what most students do not know about a normal distribution is why it is important in the study of statistics, or why we place so much emphasis upon it. So, let's see if we can acquaint ourselves somewhat with this loveliest of all forms, come to grips with it, and finally come to realize why it plays such an important, nurturing role in the lives of all researchers and statisticians.

First of all, it should be noted that there is nothing really "normal" about a normal distribution; concomitantly, there is nothing "abnormal" about data that do not distribute themselves in the shape of the normal distribution. In fact, *most distributions are NOT normal distributions!* Let me repeat: most distributions are *not* normal distributions! Distributions of populations that do tend to be normal are, for example, the heights of a large number of adult males, the weights of a large number of adult females (or males, for that matter), the dress or coat or shoe sizes of a large number of adult males or females, etc. Most importantly, from a statistical viewpoint, the frequency distribution of means of random samples of the same size always forms a normal distribution. This last sentence will undoubtedly cause considerable confusion among the ranks at this point, but again I ask you to fear not! We shall approach this notion gently and gingerly, so that shortly you too will understand what this statement means. But first, we must establish some additional guidelines for you. We shall then return to that fascinating fact that the means of random samples of the same size distribute themselves normally.

First, let us look at the characteristics of any normal distribution. A normal distribution is:

a)  symmetrical (i.e., it is divided into two equal halves by the mean of the distribution);

b)  bell-shaped; and

c)  it is completely described by its mean and its standard deviation.

We should note that although we sometimes get the idea that there is only one kind of normal distribution, and draw diagrams as if that were so, there really are all kinds of normal distributions. Some may have very little variability, and are therefore rather thin and tall; others, with a great deal of variability, are sort of short and fat and spread out:

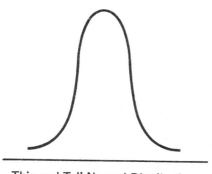

Thin and Tall Normal Distribution

Short, Fat, and Spread Out Normal Distribution

But all of them have the characteristics outlined above. So, what does it mean when we say that a normal distribution is completely described by its mean and its standard deviation? It means that, knowing the mean and the standard deviation of any normal distribution, we can draw that distribution as a frequency polygon; furthermore, we can know exactly what percentage of cases falls where, and thereby also know where any specific case lies in relation to the entire population. Let us look at a normal distribution and see what this means.

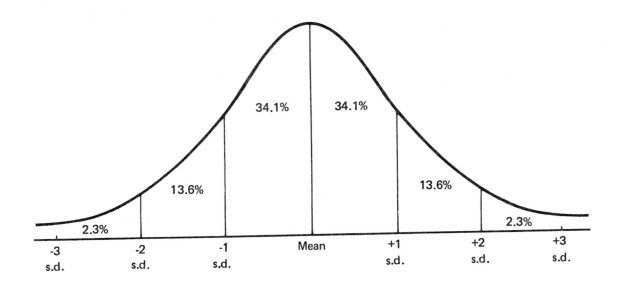

In the diagram above, the central dividing line is at the mean; +1 s.d., +2 s.d., and +3 s.d. indicate the distances of 1, 2, and 3 standard deviations from the mean in one direction (the positive one), while –1 s.d., etc., indicate the distance of 1, 2, and 3 standard deviations from the mean in the other direction (the negative one). The percentage figures indicate the distribution of cases in *any and all* normal distributions. In other words, in all normal distributions, 34.1 percent of all cases fall between the mean and +1 standard deviation; equally, 34.1 percent of all cases fall between the mean and –1 standard deviation; an additional 13.6 percent lie between 1 and 2 standard deviations from the mean; and only a miserable little 2.3 percent fall beyond 2 deviations away from the mean. With only minimal addition or subtraction (you all remember how to do that?) we could also say that 68.2 percent of all cases fall within the range of plus or minus 1 standard deviation from the mean, and that approximately 95 percent of all cases fall between –2 and +2 standard deviations from the mean.

So what? Let's see what happens if we apply this to specific cases. Suppose we have a normal distribution of test scores for 135,247 students, where the mean score is 100, and the standard deviation is 20. Your kid comes home and reports that the teacher told him that he received a score of 140 on that test. My kid comes home, and tells me that he received a score of 60 on that test. How well or poorly did each of them do in comparison to the rest of the students? Let us look at what we know about the distribution of these scores.

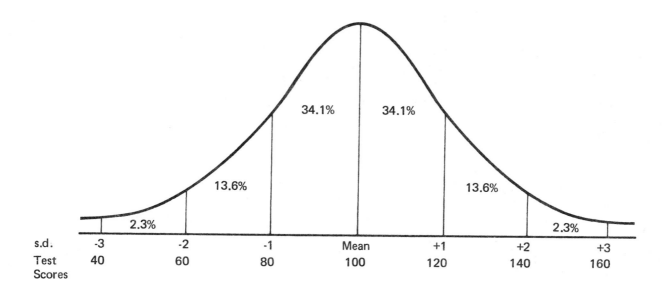

| s.d. | -3 | -2 | -1 | Mean | +1 | +2 | +3 |
| Test Scores | 40 | 60 | 80 | 100 | 120 | 140 | 160 |

If we know that the mean is 100, and the standard deviation is 20, then obviously (I hope) +1 s.d. is a score of 120, +2 s.d. is a score of 140, -1 s.d. is a score of 80, etc. If we now look at your child's score of 140, we see that he is 2 standard deviations above the mean, and we know that this indicates that only about 2.3 percent of the scores were higher than his. Or, if you like, you can say that he did better than approximately 97.7 percent of all students. My rotten kid, on the other hand, with his score of 60, is 2 standard deviations below the mean: only 2.3 percent of the scores were worse than his, while 97.7 percent of the students did better.

In all distributions, normal or not, we can take any score and, knowing the mean and standard deviation, can translate that "raw" score into the number of standard deviations above or below the mean. And that, indeed, is known as the *standard score*. In the above example, your child, with a raw score of 140, had a standard score of +2; in other words, his score was 2 standard deviations above the mean. My child, with a raw score of 60, had a standard score of -2; his score was 2 standard deviations below the mean. Only with a normal distribution, however, can we then go on to state precisely what the percentages above or below that score are.

Now, as some of you may already have surmised, life is not always as simple as in the above example. Your child and mine were both very cooperative by getting scores that were an exact number of standard deviations from the mean. But what about the children who have scores of 65, or 47, or 126? How can we say exactly where they fit in this picture? We can, at this point, approximate where they stand, but how can we state their position with exactitude, not to say rectitude? What we have to do is calculate their standard score (i.e., the number of standard deviations they are removed from the mean), and then see what percentage of cases are either above or below that score. Since all normal distributions have proportionately the same percentages in the same places, we do have a magic little table where this can be looked up. You will find this table in the Appendix, Table I, entitled "Brief Table of the Probabilities that a Given z-Score will be Exceeded." All that the phrase "z-score" means is "standard scores." But it is shorter to say z-score than to say standard score; it also sounds so much more erudite. If you look at this table, and go back to the example of our two kids, you will find that for a z-score of 2.00, the probability that this score will be exceeded is .023, or 2.3 percent. This, of course, is exactly what we had concluded previously. Since the normal distribution is symmetrical, there is no need to list both positive and negative z-scores; a standard score of +2 has the same probability of being exceeded as a standard score of –2. The thing to note, however, is that this notion of "being exceeded" indicates how much of the distribution is left in the tail end of our normal curve, going in the same direction as the standard score. For example, with a z-score of +2, the percentage of cases exceeding that is 2.3 percent; i.e., there are 2.3 percent of cases that did *better*. With a z-score of –2, on the other hand, 2.3 percent of the cases did *worse*.

Now that you understand all that, let's go back to the question we asked previously: How can one transform raw scores into z-scores (or standard scores)? Very simple. We subtract the mean from the raw score, and divide by the standard deviation. That is really what we did before — we took your child's score of 140, subtracted the mean of 100 from it (that gave us 40), then divided by the standard deviation, which was 20, and got a z-score of 2. We did not actually have to perform this complicated operation in that case, because it was so obvious. But what if your child's score is 130? In that case we would say:

$$\text{standard score} = \frac{\text{raw score} - \text{mean}}{\text{stand. dev.}} = \frac{130 - 100}{20} = \frac{30}{20} = 1.5$$

The z-score for that case, then, is 1.5, and if we look that up on our magic table, we find that the probability that that score will be exceeded is .067, or 6.7 percent. In other words, 6.7 percent of the cases did *better* than your child (i.e., their scores were higher than 130).

Let's take another example: suppose we have a child who received a score of 65 on the test. What does this mean? Well, to calculate his z-score, we say:

$$z = \frac{65 - 100}{20} = \frac{-35}{20} = -1.75$$

The minus sign tells us that we are going in the opposite direction than we went before, and the table of z-scores, therefore, is going to tell us the percentage of cases who did *worse* than this one. If we now look up 1.75 on the table, we don't find it (this is a *brief* table, remember). We do know from the table, however, that a z-score of 1.7 = a probability of .045, and that a z-score of 1.8 = a probability of .036, and we can therefore approximate that a z-score of 1.75 must be around .04. We then conclude that approximately 4 percent of cases fall *below* a score of 65. Or, if we like, we can then subtract these 4 percent from the total 100 percent and say that 96 percent of the kids did better on this test than the poor soul with a score of 65.

One important word of caution: Remember, *you can only do this if you have a normal distribution!*

I realize that there are many questions which we have still not answered, and many new ones we have raised: for example, what is this concept of "probability"? What happens with samples of populations? What about cases where we do not have a numerical mean, but deal with proportions (e.g., 60 percent of all college students are male)? What in hell was the meaning of that cryptic statement that the means of all possible samples of the same size distribute themselves in the form of a normal distribution? If you really want to know, tune in next week at the same time, when we shall present the next chapter of "Batman, Fu-Man-Chu, and Captain Marvel Lost in the Statistical Realms."

## PRACTICE SHEETS

1. Using the magic table in the Appendix, determine what the probability is that the following z-scores will be exceeded.

   a)   1.0

   b)   3.0

   c)   –1.28

   d)   2.45

   e)   –1.96

   f)   2.32

   g)   –1.80

   h)   2.60

   i)   2.10

   j)   –.50

2. In a normal distribution, what proportion of cases fall between the following z-scores?

   a)   .4 to 1.5

   b)   .4 to –1.5

   c)   0 to .1

   d)   1 to 1.1

   e)   2 to 2.1

   f)   1.96 to –1.96

   g)   2.32 to –2.32

   h)   –1.5 to 3.0

   i)   2.0 to –3.0

   j)   1.6 to 3.0

For each of the following problems, draw a pretty diagram of the normal distribution, label the base line both in terms of z-scores and raw scores, and answer the questions.

3. You have a normal distribution of the heights of women, with a mean of 65 inches and a standard deviation of 3 inches.

   a)   What proportion of women will be below 62 inches? Above 62 inches?

   b)   What proportion will be above 68 inches? Below 68 inches?

   c)   What proportion will be above 71 inches? Below 71 inches?

   d)   What proportion will be below 58 inches? Above 58 inches?

   e)   What proportion will be between 60 and 69 inches? Between 67 and 72 inches?

4. The mean of a normal distribution is 80, and its standard deviation is 10.

   What is the standard score for each of the following values, and what proportion of cases fall above and below the following values?

   a)   90

   b)   110

   c)   65

   d)   58

   e)   75

   f)   80

   g)   103

   h)   68

   i)   71

   j)   95

63

5. You have a normal distribution of weights of men, with a mean of 160 lbs. and a standard deviation of 20 lbs.

   a) What proportion are between 140 and 180 lbs?

   b) Between 120 and 200 lbs?

   c) Above 200 lbs?

   d) Below 150 lbs?

   e) What weight has 95% above it?

   f) 95% below it?

   g) Between what weights do the middle 50% fall?

   h) The middle 75%?

   i) The middle 99%?

   j) The heaviest 10%?

# CHAPTER 8
# A BRIEF INTRODUCTION TO SAMPLING
# AND TO WHERE IT LEADS

It is not the purpose of this epic to present a detailed analysis of sampling procedures. For these, I refer you to some other text dealing with research methodology generally. All we shall attempt to present here is the mere skeletal knowledge and understanding you will need in order to deal with the minimum of statistical material necessary.

## SAMPLING

Until now, we have dealt primarily with descriptive statistics of entire populations. Most of the time, however, in the real world, we deal with samples, and are then not only interested in the particular group we are studying, but want to know whether we can generalize what we have found regarding this group to a larger population; we are only interested in the specific group under study to the extent that this group somehow "represents" that larger group. The small group we are studying is merely a sample of that larger group.

If we forget all about statistics and research, and just look at the way in which we go about making everyday decisions in life, we see that really we go through a research process continuously: we gather data from limited samples, try to analyze these data; draw conclusions and generalizations from them, and then guide our future actions accordingly. Essentially, this is the way we learn. Sometimes this is a rather easy process — the "data" are easy to obtain, and the conclusions we draw are applicable to a wide range of phenomena. Most of us learn at a rather tender age that fire is hot, for example. Aside from over-anxious mothers who yell, "Hot, hot! Don't touch!", we also sometimes gather these data "first hand," and find out that, yes indeed, fire is hot. This then becomes so generalizable a fact, that we consider it magic or fakery when we witness "fire-eaters" or "fire-walkers."

At other times, however, the data we gather are not so reliable, and prove to be not so generalizable: "Listen, Cynthia, not all men are like that." Are most men like that? Well, some men are like that. But what the hell does that mean? That means that poor Cynthia is going to have to get herself a larger sample or use a different sampling technique before she can generalize her experiences to the larger population of men in general.

Getting away from Cynthia and back to the purpose of this chapter, it might help if we outlined the various kinds of samples that are used in research. Essentially, there are two types of samples — non-probability (non-random) samples, and random (probability) samples.

## Non-probability samples

Non-probability samples are the kinds of samples in which everyone in the population does not have an equal chance of being included, or where the probability of everyone's inclusion is not known. It is usually not possible to make precise valid generalizations from these kinds of samples, although they do serve a purpose at times. The most common kinds of non-probability samples are:

a) Convenience (accidental) samples. These consist of the individuals who are "convenient" to the researcher, or happen to be at a certain place at a certain time "accidentally." They may be friends, acquaintances, the first 50 people you meet on the street who are willing to respond to your silly questionnaire, etc.

b) Quota samples. Here there is some attempt to get a "representative" sample, and to include appropriate quotas of men, women, Blacks, Whites, Hispanics, Orientals, young ones and old ones, etc. This kind of sample does move away from a pure convenience sample, but still has the elements of convenience attached to it. Very few interviewers, for example, if working with a quota sample, will include individuals who live on the top floors of walk-up apartment buildings, or who live at the end of a dark, smelly alley. They will still go after those individuals within the quota who are easily accessible and willing to talk to them.

c) Purposive samples. There are times when we want the viewpoints of a specific group of individuals, and we may therefore purposely go out to get them. Obviously, this kind of sample information cannot be generalized to the general public, but is the viewpoint of several "experts." Some studies, for example, make use of "judges" to gather expert judgments on the appropriateness of services.

d) Available data. At times, studies deal with the kind of data that can no longer be gathered fresh (e.g., data of the past for historical studies). In these cases, of course, we have to use whatever data are available; but we should not fool ourselves into thinking that these data are necessarily very reliable. For example, even a random study of an agency's records over the past year is not a random study at all, because it includes only those pieces of written information which workers thought worthy of including in a written record, and which were then filed. Similarly, when we think of history, it is sometimes helpful to remember that all history books (and generally most books) were written by individuals who knew how to read and write — and until very recently, this automatically excluded the poor. Yes, Algernon, History is a biased sample!

## Random (Probability) Samples

What is really meant by a random sample is that the process by which the sample was obtained was random. Essentially, in a random sample, every item in the population must have an equal chance of being included in the sample, and the process by which the sample is chosen (since there is usually a large number of different samples possible) must be a random, non-biased process.

a) Simple random samples. You are all familiar with choosing random samples, as when names are pulled out of a hat. Usually, this is not a very satisfactory process for choosing large samples. It is much more satisfying to enter a table of random numbers. Almost every research and statistics book has at its end at least one page of random numbers — and so does this one! After several random procedures (such as coin tossing) you arrive at a starting point in your table of random numbers, and then, by matching the random numbers with numbers previously assigned to your cases, you end up with a random selection of cases — a random sample.

b) Systematic random samples. At other times it is possible and simpler, to take a "systematic sample." Let us assume, for example, that you want to arrive at a sample of 200 out of 1,000 students. If the names are arranged in alphabetical order, you could then, after having picked the first individual by a random process, go on to choose every fifth student, and thus arrive at your sample of 200 students. It is important to note, however, that in many cases there is some question as to how random a systematic sample is, and unless the savings in time, money and effort are considerable, it is advisable to use the table of random numbers. Most importantly, one must not use a systematic sampling technique if the items to be sampled are already arranged in some kind of systematic way. For example, if we wish to do a study of the family income of the residents of a certain community of home owners, the best way of going about drawing a sample would be to use the table of random numbers, after having assigned each house in that community a number of its own. The reason for *not* using a systematic sample in this case is that the houses on a block are arranged according to a system: the corner houses are bigger and more expensive than the houses in the middle of the block, and consequently chances are that the residents of the corner houses are more affluent than the residents of the middle-of-the-block homes. Suppose we try a systematic sample on every fifth house, and suppose the homes are usually arranged 10 to a block: if my random starting number is home #5, my sample will look as follows:

5, 10, 15, 20, 25, 30, 35, 40, etc.

In other words, exactly *half* of my sample will be composed of corner houses, which will give me a totally misleading view of the affluence of this community. If, on the other hand, my random starting number was home #3, my sample would look as follows:

3, 8, 13, 18, 23, 28, 33, 38, 43, 48, etc.

In effect, I would *never* hit a corner house, and would arrive at an equally misleading picture of this community. I hope it is therefore clear why you can only use a systematic sample if the original population is not systematized in any way.

c) Stratified random samples. This type of sample represents a combination of the quota sampling technique and random sampling procedures. There are times when we think that certain characteristics of the population should be proportionately represented in our sample. A simple or a systematic random sample will certainly not guarantee that our sample represents the population along these characteristics, except when we do have a fairly large sample. What can be done to assure ourselves of both the representativeness and the randomness of our sample, is to first divide the population into different groups (strata) along these characteristics, and then to sample randomly from within each of these strata, in accordance with the proportionate number in each stratum.

For example, if we are conducting a study of student attitudes toward the "sexual revolution," and planning on a sample of 100 students, we might want to make sure that we have both male and female students represented proportionately within our final sample. In order to accomplish this, we can take the Registrar's list of students, and first divide these into male and female students. Let us assume that out of our list of 10,000 students, 6,000 are women and 4,000 are men. Having divided the students into these two strata (male and female), we can now take a one-percent random sample of each stratum, resulting in a sample of 60 female and 40 male students. Please note that although similar to a quota sample, in this case the final sampling process is a random process. Similar procedures can be employed to create more and more strata, but the final sampling process within each stratum must be random.

d) Cluster sampling. This technique is also known as multi-stage sampling, and is most useful with large samples, or survey studies, or in instances in which it is impossible to enumerate the population. For example, if we wanted to do a national study of seventh graders' attitudes toward stealing, we could start with a listing of all counties within the United States, and draw a random sample of counties. Within each of the counties selected, we could then draw a random sample of school districts. Within each of the selected school districts, we would randomly select a number of schools that have seventh graders in them. Within each of the schools, we would randomly select a number of seventh grade classes, and the students in these classes would finally be the sample of our study.

These, essentially, are the basic types of sampling techniques, presented in their simplest form. Frequently, in any one study, combinations of these techniques, or further elaborations of them are employed, but we will not delve into the types of samples any further.

## THE SAMPLING DISTRIBUTION OF MEANS

Since random samples are the results of random processes, the probability of a certain sample value coming up can be calculated. Let us see what this means, first from a purely common-sense viewpoint.

Suppose we have a class, in which the ages of the students are as follows:

5, 5, 6, 6, 6, 6, 7, 7, 7, 7, 7, 7, 7, 7, 8, 8, 8, 8, 9, 9 years

The mean age of this group is 7 years. Suppose we start picking random samples of 3 children. Some of these samples will consist of extreme cases only — like a sample of 5, 5, 6, years; or 8, 9, 9, years — and if we did not know the true mean of this population, these samples would give us misleading results (in one case, we would conclude that the mean is 5.3 years; in the other extreme case, we would conclude that the mean is 8.7 years). But if you could visualize all the possible samples of three that could be drawn from this population, I hope you would realize that the chance of picking such extreme samples is pretty small; many more of our samples would consist of, for example:

7, 7, 7, years — mean = 7 years;
6, 7, 7 years — mean = 6.7 years;
7, 7, 8 years — mean = 7.3 years;
6, 6, 8 years — mean = 6.7 years; etc.

This just makes common sense — there are more 6, 7, and 8 year olds in this class to be part of our sample of 3, than there are 5 and 9 year olds. Even if we get combinations of extreme scores like 5, 5, 9 years (mean = 6.3 years), or 5, 9, 9 years (mean = 7.6 years), they tend to approach the mean of the total group, which is 7 years. What we can say, therefore, just on the basis of common sense, is that the sample means will tend to cluster aroung the mean of the original population; concomitantly, we also have the notion that extreme differences from the population mean will be rare. One other concept which should have emerged out of the dim recesses of your mind during the above discussion, is that even though the population mean was 7 years, many samples of that population will *not* have the mean of exactly 7 years.

Again, we can relate all of the above information to our everyday experiences; but I do not wish us to return to poor Cynthia. Instead, let us go on to more worthy spheres of endeavor. As we have already hinted, the way in which these sample means will distribute themselves if we go through an infinite sampling process (i.e., we take a sample, get its mean, throw it back — infinitely), tends to be in the form of a normal distribution; the means of all samples of the same size will tend to cluster around the population mean, but will vary from each other. In other words, they have variability, and this variability is really the standard deviation of the sample means around the population mean. This kind of a standard deviation is usually called the *standard error of the mean.* But remember what this means: it means, really, the standard deviation (or average deviation) of the means of all possible samples of the same size from the true population mean. Now, in an original population, we could say that the standard deviation was determined by how much deviation there was in that original population; you remember, no doubt, the concept of deviation being the opposite of clustering. But here, in this mythical world of "all possible samples," what determines the size of the standard error? Now, again, to our common sense model:

a) Certainly, the variability in the original population must play a role in this. If there is no variability in the original population, I can't get any variability into the samples; i.e., if all the kids in the class are 7 years old, there is no way in which I can possibly draw a sample that will give me a mean other than 7 years. On the other hand, if there is a great deal of variability in the original population, I can expect some reflection of this in my samples.

b) It also makes sense that samples of a larger size will have less variability than small samples. In the class which we used as an example earlier in this chapter, we had the following distribution of ages:

5, 5, 6, 6, 6, 6, 7, 7, 7, 7, 7, 7, 7, 7, 8, 8, 8, 8, 9, 9 years.

Suppose we picked samples of 2: what are the most extreme sample means we could obtain? A sample of 5 years and 5 years would give us a sample mean of 5 years, while a sample at the other extreme (a sample of the two 9-year olds) would give us a sample mean of 9 years. Now, that's considerable variability from the true population mean of 7 years. What happens if we enlarge our sample size to 3? What are the most extreme samples we could then obtain? As we have seen before, with samples of 3, the most extreme means we could obtain are 5.3 years and 8.7 years. Let us note, if you please, that this is some improvement over our samples of 2. Let's take it just one step further: what happens with samples of 4? The smallest possible mean you could obtain would come from the samples of 5, 5, 6, 6 years, and the mean here would be 5.5 years. The largest possible mean you could obtain would come from the sample 8, 8, 9, 9 years, and would be 8.5 years. Now, these means of 5.5 and 8.5 years are still considerably removed from the true mean of 7 years, but note that we are steadily improving as we increase the sample size. It should be noted, of course, that as we increase the sample size we will generally get more samples that will cluster around the true mean (more clustering = less variability), but here we are only trying to get you to see, in terms of common sense, that enlarging the sample size certainly cuts down the range of possible sample means. We could present this in the form of a table.

### EXTREME SAMPLE MEANS

| Sample Size | Smallest mean value possible | Largest mean value possible | True mean |
|---|---|---|---|
| 2 | 5 yrs. | 9 yrs. | 7 yrs. |
| 3 | 5.3 | 8.7 | 7 |
| 4 | 5.5 | 8.5 | 7 |
| 5 | 5.6 | 8.4 | 7 |
| 6 | 5.67 | 8.33 | 7 |
| 7 | 5.86 | 8.14 | 7 |
| 8 | 6.0 | 8.0 | 7 |
| 9 | 6.1 | 7.9 | 7 |
| 10 | 6.2 | 7.8 | 7 |

As this table indicates, increasing the sample size necessarily cuts down the possible extreme means, so that they begin to approach the true population mean. If we carried this still further, we would finally get to the point where the most extreme means with samples of 19 would be 6.9 and 7.1; that's damned little variability. We see, then, that another factor which determines variability of samples is the sample size. Stated in the form of what is called the "central limit theorem," we would say that the sampling distribution of any mean will approach normality (i.e., it will become more and more like a true normal distribution) as the sample size increases.

What we have attempted to indicate in the above is that, logically, the variability of sample means is influenced by two factors:

a)    the amount of variability in the original population, and

b)    the size of the sample.

The greater the variability in the original population, the greater the standard error of the mean; the greater the sample size, the smaller the standard error of the mean. Mathematically, the relationship is not quite so direct; actually, the formula for the standard error of the mean is:

$$\text{standard error of mean} = \frac{\text{standard dev. of orig. pop.}}{\sqrt{\text{sample size}}} = \frac{s}{\sqrt{n}}$$

What we have now are several concepts put together, and it might help to summarize them at this point.

a) All possible samples of a given size distribute themselves normally (i.e., in the form of a normal distribution) around the population mean;

b) the standard deviation of these samples (i.e., the standard error of the mean) equals the standard deviation of the original population divided by the square root of the sample size.

Let us use some brief examples to clarify this. Suppose we know that the mean age of all students at the University of Vartizhen is 22 years, and the standard deviation of that population is 2 years. What is the standard error of the mean for all samples of size 4?

$$\text{std. error of mean} = \frac{\text{std. error of orig. pop.}}{\sqrt{\text{sample size}}} = \frac{2}{\sqrt{4}} = \frac{2}{2} = 1 \text{ year}$$

What happens if we increase the sample size to 9?

$$\text{std. error of mean} = \frac{2}{\sqrt{9}} = \frac{2}{3} = .667 \text{ years}$$

And what if we increase the sample size to 25?

$$\text{std. error of mean} = \frac{2}{\sqrt{25}} = \frac{2}{5} = .40 \text{ years}$$

And if we really cracked up, and used samples of size 100, we would get:

$$\text{std. error of mean} = \frac{2}{\sqrt{100}} = \frac{2}{10} = .20 \text{ years}$$

So we see that as we increase the sample size, we do indeed decrease the standard error of the mean. *The mean itself, of course, remains the same in all of the above examples; the mean is still what it ever was, namely 22 years.*

But, you say, so what? And that is always a valid question. What follows logically, I hope, is the notion that just as we were able to interpret any individual score or value in an original population that was normally distributed, we should now be able to do the same with any sample score. This is based upon the idea that the means of all samples of a given size distribute themselves normally.

For example, let us say that you know from the latest statistics published in the *Welfare Reporter* that nationally, the mean length of time that a family is on AFDC is 24 months, and the standard deviation of that population is 10 months. You have a hunch (that's a crude hypothesis) that this is not true of the cases at the Southeast office. You take a random sample of 25 cases, and find that the mean for your sample is 20 months. How "way out" is that?

Well, let's take a look:

Sample mean = 20 months
Sample size = 25
Population mean = 24 months
Std. dev. = 10 months

$$\text{Std. error of mean} = \frac{\text{std. dev. of orig. pop.}}{\sqrt{\text{sample size}}} = \frac{10}{\sqrt{25}} = \frac{10}{5} = 2 \text{ months}$$

In other words, all samples of size 25 distribute themselves as follows:

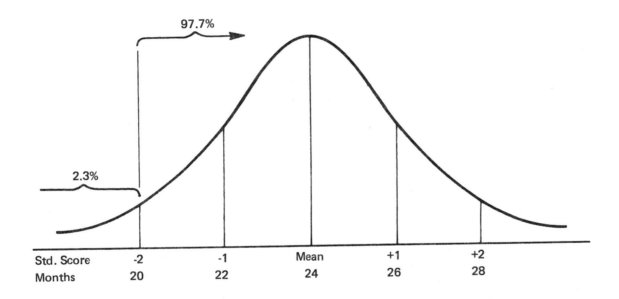

| Std. Score | -2 | -1 | Mean | +1 | +2 |
| Months | 20 | 22 | 24 | 26 | 28 |

Your sample mean was 20 months. We know, just from looking at the above diagram, that this is 2 standard deviations below the mean, and that therefore only about 2.3 percent of all means of samples of 25 would fall below 20 months. We could, of course, also say that the z-score for your sample was −2, and look this up on our dear old magic table and read the probability of .023 from it. In either case, you would conclude that, based upon your sample information, the cases at the Southeast office do seem to be quite different from the national picture, and tend to stay on AFDC for a shorter period of time.

Let us again see the impact of the sample size upon these kinds of problems. Suppose the situation were exactly the same as described above, but this time, instead of taking a sample of 25 cases, you only took 9 cases. What would happen?

72

Sample mean = 20 months
Sample size = 9
Population mean = 24 months
Std. dev. = 10 months

$$\text{Std. error of mean} = \frac{\text{std. dev. of orig. pop.}}{\sqrt{\text{sample size}}} = \frac{10}{\sqrt{9}} = \frac{10}{3} = 3.33 \text{ months}$$

In the form of a diagram, this means:

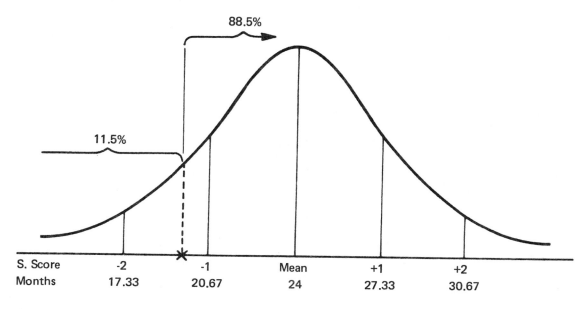

| S. Score | -2 | -1 | Mean | +1 | +2 |
|---|---|---|---|---|---|
| Months | 17.33 | 20.67 | 24 | 27.33 | 30.67 |

Our sample mean was 20 months. Again, just from looking at the normal curve, we can see that this mean is slightly more than one standard deviation below the mean of 24 months. To be more exact, we could calculate precisely where it falls, and then look up how many cases are even below it. You remember, no doubt, that when we were trying to see where an individual score fits into a normal distribution, we said that:

$$z = \frac{\text{raw score} - \text{mean}}{\text{std. dev.}}$$

Similarly now, when dealing with samples, we can say that:

$$z = \frac{\text{sample mean} - \text{pop. mean}}{\text{std. error}}$$

In this case then,
$$z = \frac{20 - 24}{3.33} = \frac{-4}{3.33} = -1.2$$

73

If we now look up a z-score of 1.2 on our table, we find a probability of .115, indicating that 11.5% of all means of sample size 9 fall even below our sample mean of 20 months. Here we might conclude that our sample is not really that "way out."

Just one more time! Let us work the same problem, assuming that you used a sample size of 100.

Sample mean = 20 months
Sample size = 100
Population mean = 24 months
Std. dev. = 10 months

$$\text{Std. error of mean} = \frac{\text{std. dev.}}{\sqrt{\text{sample size}}} = \frac{10}{\sqrt{100}} = \frac{10}{10} = 1 \text{ month}$$

The distribution, then, of all samples of size 100 would look as follows:

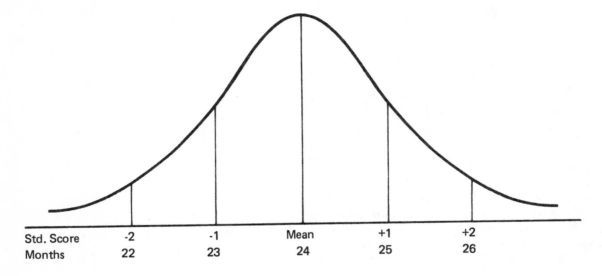

| Std. Score | -2 | -1 | Mean | +1 | +2 |
|---|---|---|---|---|---|
| Months | 22 | 23 | 24 | 25 | 26 |

Clearly, our sample mean of 20 months is so way out, that it is actually off the diagram! To calculate its position exactly, we would again say:

$$z = \frac{\text{sample mean} - \text{pop. mean}}{\text{std. error}} = \frac{20 - 24}{1} = \frac{-4}{1} = -4$$

If we now look up a z-score of 4 on our table, we find it to be .00003; in other words, only three hundredthousandths of the samples of size 100 are that "way out."

Let us try to summarize what the three examples above indicate. Remember, we left everything the same, except for the sample size.

| sample size | z-score | prob. that z exceeded | conclusion reached |
|---|---|---|---|
| 9 | 1.2 | .115 | our sample not really different from population |
| 25 | 2.0 | .023 | our sample does seem to be different from total population |
| 100 | 4.0 | .00003 | our sample very definitely is "way out," and different from the total population |

The point at which you decide that your sample is, indeed, different from the total population, will be dealt with in the near future. The purpose of the above tabulation is merely to point out the impact of the sample size upon the standard error of the mean, and consequently upon any conclusions that are reached. What we have established, I hope, is the notion that by using sample information and the standard error of the mean, we can place any sample mean into a normal distribution, and thereby determine just how "way out" our sample results are.

## PROPORTIONS

One of the areas that we have thus far carefully avoided (not to say skirted) deals with proportions. How can we apply what we have said thus far to the kind of nominal data we sometimes get, which state, for example, that the proportion of red-heads is 20 percent, or that 60 percent of all students at State University are female?

First, let us cover some simple vocabulary. We frequently speak of such proportional data in terms of "successes" and "failures." What these terms refer to is whether or not any individual member of the population or sample exhibits the characteristic you are looking for. If we are dealing with a study of the proportion of red-heads at BOXU, for example, then every time you hit a red-head, that's a "success" (somehow, that doesn't sound very good, but I hope you get the point); every time you hit somebody who is not a red-head, that's a "failure."

When we discussed other types of numerical data in some of the previous chapters, it made sense to talk of means, medians, and modes, and of standard deviations in original populations. It obviously makes no sense to speak of data that deal with proportions in these terms; nor can we visualize a "normal" distribution of some proportions within a population. When we get to samples, however, we can see that the concept of the standard error of the mean does make some sense for proportions as well. If, for example, our total population of hair color among BOXU students resulted in 20 percent red-heads, we can see that drawing repeated samples of, say, 100 students, will give us results very closely analogous to what happened with means; i.e., most of the samples will cluster around the population value of 20 percent red-heads, some will be slightly removed from that 20 percent figure, and a few samples will give us really extreme results. Here again, the data of all possible samples of a given size will distribute themselves normally, with the true population proportion being the mean.

All we then have to know to describe any such population is the standard error of the mean. For proportions, the formula is:

$$\text{std. error} = \sqrt{\frac{PQ}{n}}$$

P stands for the proportion of successes; Q stands for the proportion of failures; and n is the sample size.

Thus, for example, if the proportion of red-heads in the original population is 20 percent (or .20) and the sample size is 25, then the standard error for all possible samples of size 25 is:

$$\sqrt{\frac{PQ}{n}} = \sqrt{\frac{(.20)(.80)}{25}} = \sqrt{\frac{.16}{25}} = \sqrt{.0064} = .08$$

In other words, all possible samples of size 25 will distribute themselves as follows:

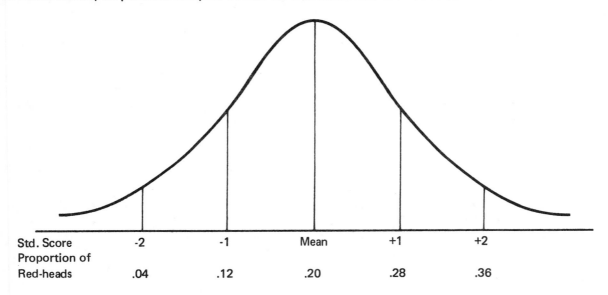

| Std. Score | -2 | -1 | Mean | +1 | +2 |
|---|---|---|---|---|---|
| Proportion of Red-heads | .04 | .12 | .20 | .28 | .36 |

Once we have our dear old normal curve back, we can then go on and play the same games we played in the preceding section of this chapter. For example, suppose that the above data regarding 20 percent red-heads come from a nation-wide study of college students. Looking cursorily at the students of BOXU, you form a hypothesis which says that at BOXU the proportion of red-heads is more than 20 percent, and you draw a random sample of 25 students to test your hypothesis. Of your sample of 25 students, 7 are red-heads. Are the students in your sample different from the national population of students? I know you can hardly wait to find out, so let's move right along:

Population proportion = .20          Sample proportion = $\frac{7}{25}$ = .28

Standard error for samples of 25 = .08 (we figured that out above)

Just from looking at the distribution of all samples of size 25 above, you should be able to see that we are exactly 1 standard deviation above the mean (or, that we have a standard score of 1). Looking this up on our table, we find that 15.9 percent of all samples of size 25 lie even beyond this. So, we cannot really conclude that our sample was that different from the national picture.

Again, of course, the sample size plays a crucial role. Let us say that instead of a sample of 25, you had taken a sample of 125, of whom 35 were red-heads (the same 28 percent as before). What conclusions would you have come to?

$$\text{Sample proportion} = .28$$
$$\text{Sample size} = 125$$
$$\text{Population proportion} = .20$$

$$\text{Std. error} = \sqrt{\frac{PQ}{n}} = \sqrt{\frac{(.20)\,(.80)}{125}} = \sqrt{\frac{.16}{125}} = \sqrt{.00128} = .035$$

The distribution of all samples of size 125, then would look as follows:

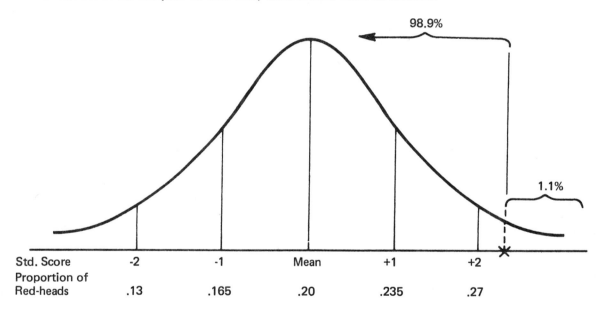

| Std. Score | -2 | -1 | Mean | +1 | +2 |
|---|---|---|---|---|---|
| Proportion of Red-heads | .13 | .165 | .20 | .235 | .27 |

Again, from just looking at the distribution of all samples of size 125, we could see that our sample proportion of .28 is more than 2 standard deviations above the mean. To find the z-score exactly, we would say:

$$z = \frac{\text{sample proportion} - \text{pop. proportion}}{\text{std. error}} \quad \text{or}$$

$$z = \frac{p - P}{\text{std. error}} = \frac{.28 - .20}{.035} = \frac{.08}{.035} = 2.29 \text{ or approx. } 2.3$$

In other words, our sample proportion is 2.3 standard deviations above the population proportion (i.e., it has a z-score of 2.3). If we now look this z-score up on the table, we find that the probability of that score being exceeded is only .011; only about 1 percent of all samples would give us an even higher proportion of red-heads than we got in our sample. Here you would conclude that our sample is quite different from what we would have expected, and that there does seem to be a higher proportion of red-heads at BOXU than is true nationally. What you then do with this little bit of fascinating information is, of course, dependent upon how you feel about red-heads.

I realize that we still have not come to grips with the concept of probability, although we have been dropping some hints in that direction. If you can continue to bear with us, we shall, hopefully, start putting some of this material together further and further and further anon.

# PRACTICE SHEETS

1. For each of the following studies, indicate the sampling technique you would use, why you have chosen that particular technique, and how you would go about gathering your sample information.

   a) A study of the shoe sizes of students at BOXU.

   b) A study of undergraduate majors of graduate students at the School of Social Work.

   c) A study of the age distribution of clients in family service agencies throughout the country.

   d) A study to determine the best possible treatment modality for families of dying cancer patients.

   e) A study of clients' views of the effectiveness of an agency's program.

2. Ten years ago, a study was done of the ages of clients of a family service agency, and it was found that the mean age was 40 years and the standard deviation was 10 years. You think that over these past few years, the client population has become considerably younger. You take a random sample of the ages of 16 clients and find an average age of 36 years.

   a) What is the standard error of the mean for all samples of size 16? (draw a picture)

   b) What is the standard score for our sample?

   c) What proportion of samples of size 16 would give us an even younger age than 36 years?

   d) What would you conclude?

   e) Suppose you had done the same study, but had taken a sample of 36 clients. What would your responses to the above questions be then? (draw a picture)

3. In a study measuring the degree of satisfaction with statistics courses at graduate schools of social work, it was found that 30 percent were "satisfied" with the course. A study that you did here, using a random sample of 20 students, indicated that 8 out of these 20 students were "satisfied" with their course.

   a) What is the standard error of the mean for all samples of size 20? (draw a picture)

   b) What is the standard score for your sample?

   c) What is the probability that this score would be exceeded?

   d) What would you conclude?

   e) Suppose you had done the same study, but this time had taken a sample of 40 students, and had found that 16 were "satisfied" with the course. What would your answers to the above questions be then? (draw another picture)

4. A population of the test scores of 12,000 college females has a mean of 60 and a standard deviation of 10.

   a) If a random sample of 10 is drawn from this population, what is the probability of obtaining a mean of 55 or higher?

   b) If you had taken a random sample of 25, what is the probability of obtaining a mean of 55 or higher?

   c) Suppose, for some reason, you did not have the time to draw a random sample, but used a "convenience" sample instead, and increased your sample size to 100. What is the probability of obtaining a mean of 55 or higher?

5. You are given (for the population) a normal distribution of weights of men, with a mean of 160 lbs. and a standard deviation of 20 lbs. Your sample size is 36 (n = 36).

   a) What proportion of such samples will fall between 156.7 and 163.3 lbs?

   b) Between 153.3 and 166.7 lbs?

   c) Above 166.7 lbs?

   d) Below 150 lbs?

   e) What weight has 95 percent of samples above it?

   f) 95 percent below it?

   g) Between what weights do the middle 50 percent fall?

   h) The middle 75 percent?

   i) The middle 99 percent?

   j) How do these answers compare to the ones you have for Question 5, Chapter 7? Explain, please.

# CHAPTER 9
# NOW DO WE GET TO PROBABILITY? PROBABLY

Once having entered that mysterious world of samples and errors, we are caught there — and if we ever hope to go on, we have to abandon all notions of certainty, of absolutism, of really knowing, of "being 100 percent sure" of anything. All we are left with, and all we can trust are the laws and concepts of probability — probably.

Let us, therefore, take a brief glance at what this concept of probability indicates to us. This fascinating subject could easily take several chapters, and help you to win at poker, blackjack, dice, and all the other games of chance (that's why research professors are so wealthy), but, as with sampling, we shall not delve into this subject in any great detail. Again, we shall attempt to present only that information which will enable you to deal with the statistical material at hand.

## PROBABILITY

As usual, it might be helpful to forget—momentarily, at least—all about research and statistics in the academic sense, and look at what we do in everyday life. As we have pointed out before, all of life is a research process — we observe, we establish some kinds of hypotheses about our observations, we draw some tentative conclusions, we test out our conclusions, we may have to revise them on the basis of new information, etc. Without this kind of process, which really is a learning process in itself, all new learning would be almost impossible — imagine not generalizing from previous experience, but handling each occurrence as if it were unique and without precedent! So we form stereotypes, opinions, views, attitudes, prejudices, values, etc. — all based upon some previous experiences, which may be more or less valid in any given situation. Actually, with any set of observable phenomena in the social sciences, only the most prejudiced individuals would operate on the basis of absolute certainty. Even a very bigoted racist would have to admit that not *all* Blacks, Browns, Asians, Jews, Poles, Irish, etc. are lazy, stupid, over-sexed, greedy, sneaky, dirty, etc.; simultaneously, even the most ardent defender of any group would have to admit that not *all* members of this group are handsome, beautiful, intelligent, honest, etc. What we are left with, then, is a certain amount of uncertainty; a degree of unpredictability in specific events; consequently, a disquieting discomfort, which says to us, "You'll never really know!" Students frequently find this rather disheartening. We know that in many areas definite answers are not possible — in philosophy, in the realm of theories, in clinical practice, in human behavior — and we can accept some uncertainty there (although people usually want definite answers even in these areas); but in statistics, where we deal with concrete numbers, where 2 + 2 = 4 and only 4, where we have rules and regulations and formulas — here too this uncertainty? I'm afraid so; no certainty — only probability.

In life, we generally use a series of words to express this uncertainty, including: sometimes, rarely, frequently, usually, unusually, and certainly probably. In statistics, we express these degrees of uncertainty numerically in terms of probability, and probability ranges from 100 percent (or 1.00) down through 50 percent (or .50) all the way to 0 percent (or .00). Of course, the greater the probability, the more certain we are that this event will actually take place; the smaller the probability, the less likely it is that this event will occur by chance. At this point, it might help to present a sort of "translation table" to clarify the relationship (not to say correlation) between these common expressions and the numerical expressions of probability.

| Probability | General Expression | Event (without getting philosophical) |
|---|---|---|
| 1.00 | absolutely certain | there will be a tomorrow |
| .991 — .999 | very certain | there will be a sun tomorrow |
| .91 — .99 | quite sure | there will be an earth tomorrow |
| .76 — .90 | I think so | there will be people alive on earth tomorrow |
| .61 — .75 | more likely than not | most of us will be alive tomorrow |
| .40 — .60 | damned if I know | one of my sons will be home in time for dinner tonight |
| .25 — .39 | doubtful | both of my sons will be home on time for dinner tonight |
| .10 — .24 | I don't think so | it will rain in San Diego tomorrow |
| .01 — .09 | rarely | it will snow in Miami tomorrow |
| .001 — .009 | very rarely | it will not snow in Chicago all winter |
| 0.00 | impossible | all students will receive an "A" in their statistics class |

The trouble, of course, is that in real life, almost nothing is ever "absolutely certain" or "impossible"; almost everything is "probable" to some degree. As you are undoubtedly aware, this is what makes for poker games, crap games, Las Vegas, etc. But, perhaps most importantly, what we are trying to stress is that most of our decisions in life are based upon some evaluation of the *probability* of the outcomes — you never *know* for sure in advance. To make things worse, this evaluation of the probability of the outcomes is based upon incomplete information, faulty information, a small sample of all possible information, etc. That's why we make so many mistakes in life. Viewed from that perspective, it is really astounding how many marriages don't break up, how many kids relate at least somewhat to their parents, how many students do learn, and how many teachers do teach.

As we have stated before, in our realm of statistics, the same circumstances pertain: we have limited information, frequently gathered from a relatively small sample, often employing poor interviewing techniques, perhaps errors in the data analysis. Just the same, we are often asked to make some prediction — to come to some conclusion (definitive, preferably) about some part of this universe out there. And really we can't. All we can ever say is what the probability is of getting the results we did get, taking into account the conditions under which we got these results. Then somebody else has to make up his mind whether this "evidence" is good enough for him or not.

Putting it another way, those of you who play poker know that a flush beats one pair, because it's harder to get a flush than it is to get a pair. Stating this another way, we would say that given a randomized deck of cards (they've been shuffled thoroughly), the probability (or the chances, or the odds) of pulling a hand with a flush is *smaller* than that of pulling a hand with one pair; certainly, the probability of getting a full house is even smaller, which is why a full house beats a flush. In the most simplified form of poker (you are playing all by yourself, and just dealing yourself five cards), the probability of getting a pair is .42, the probability of getting a flush is .002, and the probability of getting a full house is .0014. In other words, in the long run (that means if you dealt yourself an infinite number of hands) approximately 42 percent of all hands would have one pair in them, only two out of every 1,000 hands (on the average) would turn up a flush, and only 14 out of 10,000 hands (on the average) would result in a full house. Suppose now, that you are in a poker game, and one of the players gets a full house. Is he cheating? I don't know. Suppose he gets two full houses in a row. Is he cheating? Three full houses, four full houses, five full houses, . . . At which point do you decide that he is indeed cheating? Obviously, the probability of even getting two full houses in a row is extremely small; and yet, it is still within the realm of possibility. In fact, it is possible, although extremely, extremely, extremely unlikely, that someone may even get four or five full houses in a row. So, when do you decide that he's cheating? Well, other factors now come into play: is this your best friend, whom you've known to be the model of honesty all your life, or is it some shady-looking character whom nobody really knows? Also, what will be the consequences of your decision? Are you going to stand up and say, "You dirty, filthy s.o.b., you're cheating!", or are you merely going to bow out of the game politely, claiming a sudden attack of Ichthyophthirius multifilius? Obviously, all these and many other factors will have a deciding influence upon how much "proof" you really need before you decide that he is indeed cheating, and before you decide what you are going to do about it. And really, you'll never know.

That's life!

But what are we doing with this in a book on statistics? Well, I hope that the concept beginning to emerge is that when very rare events take place (three full houses in a row), we begin to suspect that something other than pure chance is operating (i.e., the guy is cheating). And, connecting this with what we have said in the previous chapter, it should begin to dawn upon you that when a sample mean is "way out" from where the population mean is (say, 2 standard deviations removed), we begin to suspect that something other than chance is operating — maybe our group really *is* different.

This topic is sometimes referred to as "Statistical Inference," since what we essentially do is to attempt to infer what the world out there is really like, merely from a sample of that world. Of course, what should again be emphasized here is that because this entire system is purely "probabilistic," it is all the more important that we try not to introduce additional sources of error by sloppy sampling, poorly constructed interview schedules, or inappropriate data analysis techniques.

## STATISTICAL INFERENCE

What we have been discussing in terms of probability, and poker, and making decisions as to whether or not Jesse James cheats at cards, may be more formally stated in research and statistical language. But basically, please remember, the concepts are the same; only their names have been changed to protect the innocent. Some of these basic concepts are:

### Hypotheses

By this time, you are undoubtedly familiar with hypotheses. Essentially, a hypothesis (the plural ends in "es") is a sort of educated hunch — a little bit more than just a wild guess, but certainly less than certain knowledge. It is based upon previous studies, your observations, what others have told you, your prejudices, values, feelings, etc. We divide hypotheses logically into two types — null hypotheses ($H_o$) and alternative hypotheses (H).

### The Null Hypothesis

This is the hypothesis that says that nothing (zero — null) is happening; it is the hypothesis of "no difference." This means that any differences that may have been observed between two populations or two different samples were purely due to natural, random, chance fluctuations, and not due to any *real* difference. In research, we assume that it is the null hypothesis which is true, unless and until we present sufficient proof that it is not true; how much proof is "sufficient proof" we shall discuss shortly.

### The Alternative Hypothesis

This is the one that says that something other than chance is really going on there — that these differences are "real," and not just due to chance. There are two types of alternative hypotheses:

a)  **Directional Hypotheses.** This is the kind of hypothesis where you are willing to say that A is better than B, or that the students at State University really are more . . . than students elsewhere, etc. Note that with directional hypotheses you are willing to say that there is a difference, *and* specify the direction of that difference.

b)  **Non-Directional Hypotheses.** With this kind of hypothesis you are willing to state that a difference does exist, but are not ready to stick your neck out to specify in what direction the difference is. You are merely saying that there is a difference between A and B, but are not willing to state that your hypothesis is that A is better than B.

Now, to where does all this lead? I have a series of possible hypotheses, I can never know for sure whether I am absolutely right or not (I can only know probabilities), so how can I make a decision? Well, I'll tell you; I'm glad you asked, because this leads us exactly to where we should go next. It leads us to the fascinating topic of levels of significance, and the different types of errors one can make regarding decisions. In other words, the stage we are at right now is the point at which you have some hypothesis (directional or non-directional), which you wish to test out against the null-hypothesis, and you have to muster enough "proof" to convince yourself and/or anyone else that your hypothesis is correct, and that the null hypothesis is wrong. But, again, how much "proof" is "enough proof"? Let us say that, generally, when your sample information casts only "little" doubt upon the null hypothesis, we would continue to accept the null hypothesis, and reject your alternative hypothesis. If, on the other hand, your sample information casts a "tremendous amount" of doubt upon the null hypothesis, then we would reject the null hypothesis, and accept the alternative hypothesis. But, you say, how much doubt is "little doubt," and how much doubt is "tremendous doubt"? And again I say unto you: there is no simple answer; it all depends upon what is involved, what the consequences of rejecting the null hypothesis are, etc.

Perhaps a little fable will help.

## FABLE

Once upon a time (all fables start that way, you know), there was a great, big, beautiful brown bear, who lived deep in the forest in the coziest, snuggiest, most comfortable of all caves. He lived there all alone, and this bothered him at times. The cave was so big, so cozy, so snug, so warm; and he knew that out there in the forest there were other animals, who were often cold and uncomfortable and wet. Also, if the truth be known, this great, big, beautiful brown bear was underneath it all a rather pusilanimous pussycat — he was afraid of being alone in the dark, and whenever it stormed, he would cower most cowardly in the furthest corner of the cave, in the fetal position, praying most fervently for the storm to subside. At times like this, he would have given almost anything just to have another beastly soul around. So he was most anxious to share his cozy, snug cave with another animal of the forest. But with whom? "Well," he thought to himself, "I am a great, big, beautiful brown bear, and I have the coziest, snuggiest, most comfortable cave in the forest. Besides that, there are a lot of things that scare the living daylights out of me. So, whoever will share my cave must prove that he is brave."

After having come to this conclusion, the brown bear put an ad in the "Burrows, Caves and Trees to Share" section of the classified pages of the "Forest News," which read:

> Cavemate wanted to share coziest,
> snuggiest ca. in fo.; species
> irrelevant, but must be friendly,
> love brown bears, and above all,
> *must be brave.* If interested,
> apply in person at Cave 491, Sun.
> after 10 A.M.

Sure enough, by 10 AM on Sunday morning, a multitude of animals had lined up before the brown bear's cave, all eager to share his famously cozy, snug cave with him. As the brown bear looked over the applicants, he could see that some of them were undoubtedly brave — there was a lion, a tiger, even a few wolves and wolverines — but the thought of sharing a cave with one of them was as frightening as being alone. So he quickly sent them away. This still left a goodly number of applicants, including a raccoon, some deer, a fox, and some rabbits. Turning to the raccoon, who was first in line, the brown bear said, "I shall be happy to share my cozy, snug cave with you, but only if you are brave." "I am brave, I am brave, I am even courageous, fearless, valiant, and bold," replied the raccoon, and he was ready to move in right then and there. "But wait," said the brown bear, "You have to prove to me that you really are brave, courageous, fearless, valiant, and bold." "How, how, how?" asked the anxious raccoon. "By performing a few tasks, which will test your bravery," and here the brown bear pulled out a copy of the WOBS (Wise Owl Bravery Scale), a 46-item performance scale which includes items such as: "Pluck out 3 eagle's feathers," "Twist a tiger's tail," "Bring back 5 hairs from a lion's . . .," etc. "O.K.; no problem," said the raccoon, as he took off into the forest — never to be heard from again.

To this very day, it is not known whether the raccoon perished while trying to accomplish one of these tasks, or whether he just decided that the whole thing wasn't worth that much bother after all. Above all, to this very day, no one knows whether he really was brave, courageous, fearless and bold, or not; the brown bear does not know either.

After waiting for several months for the raccoon to return, the brown bear realized that maybe he had made a mistake. So he looked outside the cave to see if any applicants were still left. The deer were gone; so was the fox; in fact, the only one left was a little rabbit. Now, the brown bear did not want to be alone any longer — the nights were getting darker and darker, the storm season was just around the corner, the winds were beginning to howl — but still, he wanted someone who was brave. SOOOOOOO: the brown bear called in the little rabbit and said, "I shall be happy to share my cozy, snug cave with you, but only if you are brave." "Well, I am not exactly a coward, as rabbits go," replied the little rabbit. "Wonderful, wonderful; I believe you, I believe you," cried the brown bear, and the little rabbit moved into the cozy, snug cave of the big brown bear that same day, and they lived happily ever after. But to this very day, no one knows whether the little rabbit was really brave or not; above all, the brown bear himself does not know either.

## END OF FABLE

MORAL(S): 1.  You can never really know what the "truth" is; i.e., we do not know if either the raccoon or the rabbit were really brave.

2.  Not knowing, you have to decide how much proof you need to "believe." The amount of proof you need varies from situation to situation, depending upon the different circumstances. Our bear required much more proof from the raccoon than he did from the little rabbit.

3.  If you require "too much" proof to reject the null hypothesis (in this case, that they are not brave), then you are taking a chance that you might stick with the null hypothesis even if the alternative is true. In our fable, it may have been impossible for the raccoon to come up with as much proof as the bear demanded, even if he really was brave.

4.  If you are willing to settle for "too little" proof to reject the null hypothesis, then you are taking the chance of rejecting the null hypothesis and accepting the alternative, when in reality the null hypothesis may be true. With the little rabbit, our poor bear was willing to settle for mere verbal assurance of his bravery. If, in reality, the little rabbit was not brave, but merely said so in order to get into the cozy cave, then the bear made the wrong decision regarding his hypothesis.

5.  If, of course, the raccoon really was not brave, while the little rabbit really was brave, then the bear made the correct decision. But remember —

6.  The bear will never know for certain, and neither will you. And I won't tell.

## END OF MORAL(S) OF FABLE.

Now, then, let's put all this mish-mash into research terminology. This may be most easily done if we present the various relationships between reality and decisions in the form of a little table.

|  | Reality (unknown) | |
| Decision made | Null hypothesis TRUE | Null hypothesis FALSE |
| --- | --- | --- |
| Reject null hypothesis (accept alternative) | Error Type I | Correct Decision |
| Accept null hypothesis (reject alternative) | Correct Decision | Error Type II |

What the above table indicates is that if you reject the null hypothesis when indeed the null hypothesis is false, you've made the correct decision. If, on the other hand, you reject the null hypothesis when the null hypothesis is really true, you have made an error, and this error is usually referred to as a Type I error. Concomitantly, if you accept the null hypothesis when the null hypothesis is true, you've done the right thing; but, if you accept the null hypothesis when in fact it is false, you have committed what is known as a Type II error.

The question, then, is how much of a chance you are willing to take in either direction. The amount of risk which you are willing to take of making a Type I error is known as your significance level — in other words, at that point (i.e., with that much "proof") you are willing to make the decision that your null hypothesis was wrong, and you will accept the alternative hypothesis. Again, there is no absolute significance level which is appropriate for all occasions — it all depends upon *the consequences* of accepting the alternative hypothesis. In testing medical drugs, for example, we would not put a headache remedy on the market if there is even a .01 probability that somebody would die from it; in another case, such as changing some simple form used at your agency, even if there is a probability of .30 of the new form being no better than the old one, you might still go ahead with the new form, because the consequences of your actions are not that great if you are wrong. The level of significance, then, is that probability level at which you reject the null hypothesis; you are saying that you are willing to take that much of a chance of making a Type I error.

One of the questions in your mind at this point (among others) might be, "Why not always set the level of significance so low that I'm only taking a very minute chance of making a Type I error? Why not set it at, say, .0001? Then I would only be taking 1 chance in 10,000 of accepting the alternate hypothesis when the null hypothesis is really true." That's true. But you ought to realize that you can't get something for nothing; for as you decrease the probability of making a Type I error, you are increasing the probability of making a Type II error. This is like our brown bear with the raccoon: when you expect that much proof, you might be rejecting a cavemate who is really brave; in other words, you might be rejecting the alternative hypothesis, when it is really true. This problem, which we face all the time, is called balancing the risks of error. We will not explore this any further here, except to emphasize again that you have to weigh each situation before you can make the decision as to what your level of significance shall be, and that this can only be determined by what the consequences of your decision are going to be.

## HYPOTHESIS TESTING

We are now ready to take all these concepts and put them together to test hypotheses. Hurrah! Hurrah! Hurrah!

In this next section, we will be taking some of the problems worked out in the previous chapter, but will add the concepts of probability, inference, etc., and see what we can come up with.

For example, you indubitably remember the problem which stated that nationally the mean length of time that a family is on AFDC is 24 months, and that the standard deviation of that population was 10 months. You had a hunch that this was not true of the cases at the Southeast office. You took a random sample of 25 cases and found that the mean for your sample was 20 months. The question we asked in the last chapter was, "How 'way out' is that?" Now knowing a little bit more, we can go back and restate this problem, introducing the new concepts we have been dealing with.

> **Given:**
> Population mean = 24 months
> Standard deviation = 10 months
>
> **Null Hypothesis:**
> *There is no difference* between the mean time that families are on AFDC at the Southeast office and the mean time that families are on AFDC nationally.
>
> **Possible Alternative Hypotheses:**
> 1. **Non-directional:** *there is a difference* between the mean time that families are on AFDC at the Southeast office and the mean time that families are on AFDC nationally.
> 2. **Directional:** a) the mean time that families are on AFDC at the Southeast office is *less than* the national average; or
>    b) the mean time that families are on AFDC at the Southeast office is *more than* the national average.

Let us assume that of your three different possible alternative hypotheses, you choose 2a — that the mean time that families are on AFDC at the Southeast office is less than the national average. You now have to determine what your level of significance shall be; i.e., how much of a chance of making a Type I error are you willing to take, or how much proof do you need to "believe"? That depends upon what you intend to use the information for. What will be the consequences? Are you just going to do this little study for your own interest? Well, in that case, you might settle for a significance level of .10 (i.e., you are taking a 10 percent chance of accepting your alternative hypothesis, even though the null hypothesis is really true). Or, on the other hand, are you, as Director of the Welfare Department, going to totally revise the operations of the Southeast office on the basis of the outcome of this study? Well, in that case, since so much more is at stake, you might insist upon a significance level of .01 (i.e., you are only willing to take a 1 percent chance of making a Type I error). Regardless of which level you choose, *now* is the time when you must decide; you cannot collect your data first and then decide — that's cheating, and you will fall victim to your biases and prejudices. You must decide *before you collect the data.* Let us assume, then, that for this particular case you chose a sort of moderate significance level of .05. Let's remember what this means: if the probability of your getting your sample results is *less than .05,* you will reject the null hypothesis; if the probability is *more than .05,* you will keep the null hypothesis. Remember: the smaller the probability, the better the "proof."

You now go out and gather your data. The mean for your sample of 25 cases is 20 months.

**Probability Question:**  What is the probability of getting this result or better (mean = 20 months), in a sample of this size (25 cases), if in reality the null hypothesis is true (there is no difference)?

What we did in the last chapter was to say that the standard error of the mean for all samples of

$$\text{size } 25 = \frac{\text{std. dev.}}{\sqrt{\text{sample size}}} = \frac{10}{\sqrt{25}} = \frac{10}{5} = 2 \text{ months}$$

In other words, all samples of size 25 distribute themselves as follows:

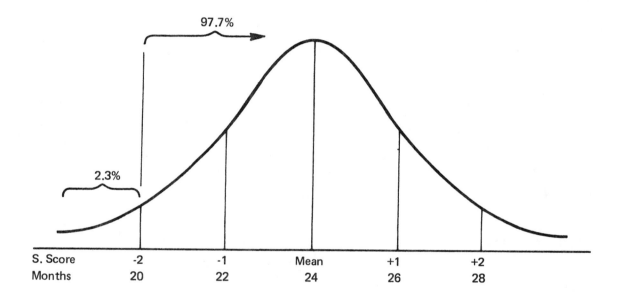

| S. Score | -2 | -1 | Mean | +1 | +2 |
|---|---|---|---|---|---|
| Months | 20 | 22 | 24 | 26 | 28 |

Our sample mean of 20 months is 2 standard deviations below the mean. The probability that this z-score would be exceeded is .023. It is therefore less than our level of significance of .05, and we would therefore *reject the null hypothesis, and accept our alternative hypothesis.* It might be helpful to remember that what we are looking for are *rare* events; if there is a considerable probability that some event is going to take place anyway, we are not impressed. Please note: "Small probabilities are beautiful!"

It might also be helpful to look at the diagram of the distribution of the means of all samples of size 25, and determine first where our level of significance lies. If we look up .05 in the "probability" column of our z-score table, we find that it corresponds to a z-score of 1.64. In other words, anything greater than a z-score of 1.64 would lead us to reject the null hypothesis in this case. Our z-score was −2.0 and, ignoring the minus sign, we see that this is more than 1.64 standard deviations from the mean. In a diagram, we might present this as follows:

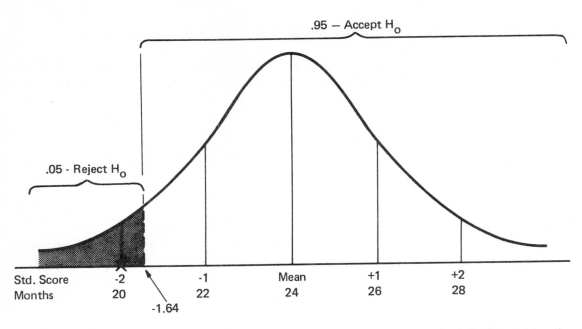

In this diagram, the 5 percent chance of error which we were willing to take is indicated by the shaded area in the left-hand tail; i.e., if our sample's mean falls within that shaded area, we will reject the null hypothesis, and accept the alternative hypothesis. If, on the other hand, our sample's mean falls within the unshaded portion of the distribution, we will keep the null hypothesis. Our sample's mean of 20 clearly turned out to fall within the shaded area (it is indicated by an X on the diagram), and therefore we will reject the null hypothesis and accept the alternative hypothesis. We conclude that: the mean time that families are on AFDC at the Southeast office is less than the national average at a .05 significance level.

Let's try another example. Suppose you know that on the XYZ National Honors Exam (to test the ability of college seniors to use left-handed pencil sharpeners), the mean score is 100, and the standard deviation is 10. Professor Timothy Kussmich, Chairman of the Admissions Committee of our School, feels that this would be an excellent test to determine whom we should admit to the school. In order to test his hypothesis that a high score on the test would be a good predictor for success at graduate school, he administers the test to a random sample of 25 students in our school. Since this test, if accepted, will replace all other entrance requirements, including the ability to breathe, Professor Kussmich realizes that much is at stake. He therefore sets his level of significance at .001. The test is then administered to our 25 students, and their mean score is 107. What does Professor Kussmich do with his hypothesis? Well, let's see:

Population mean: 100          Sample mean: 107
Population standard deviation: 10          Sample size: 25

Null Hypothesis:
    These 25 students will not do "significantly" better on this test than the national average.
Alternative Hypothesis:
    These 25 students will do "significantly" better on this test than the national average.
Significance level: .001

Probability Question:

What is the probability of getting a mean of 107 in a sample of 25 students, when, in fact, the null hypothesis is true (i.e., there is no difference between these 25 students and the national average)?

$$\text{Standard error of the mean} = \frac{\text{std. dev.}}{\sqrt{n}} = \frac{10}{\sqrt{25}} = \frac{10}{5} = 2$$

This indicates that all samples of size 25 would distribute themselves as follows:

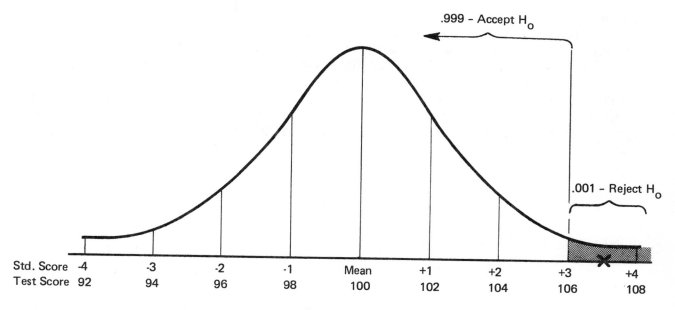

We can see immediately from the magnificent diagram above, that our sample is more than 3 standard deviations above the mean. To be more exact, we would say:

$$z = \frac{\text{sample mean} - \text{pop. mean}}{\text{std. error}} = \frac{107 - 100}{2} = \frac{7}{2} = 3.5$$

When we look up a z-score of 3.5, we find it corresponds to a probability of .0002. Since a z-score of 3 corresponds to a probability of .001, and our z-score of 3.5 indicates even less than a p of .001, Professor Kussmich rejects his null hypothesis, accepts his alternative hypothesis, and henceforth the XYZ National Honors Exam in the use of left-handed pencil sharpeners becomes the sole admission criterion for this school.

The same procedure, of course, is followed when we deal with proportions. At the end of the last chapter, we used the example of knowing that the proportion of red-heads at colleges nationally is 20 percent or .20. Your hypothesis was that there are more red-heads at BOXU, and your sample of 25 students resulted in 7 red-heads. Since this was a study of no earth-shaking significance, you might have set your significance level at .10; in other words, you are willing to take a 10 percent chance of making a Type I error. We calculated that the standard error was:

$$\text{std. error (for proportions)} = \sqrt{\frac{PQ}{n}} = \sqrt{\frac{(.2)\,(.8)}{25}} = \sqrt{\frac{.16}{25}} = \sqrt{.0064} = .08$$

The standard score for our sample, then, would be:

$$z = \frac{.28 - .20}{.08} = \frac{.08}{.08} = 1$$

If we now look up a z-score of 1, we find that this is still exceeded by 15.9 percent of all samples of size 25, and we would therefore regretfully conclude that even with our relatively liberal significance level of .10, we would have to reject the alternative hypothesis, and keep the null hypothesis: our students are not really different from the national average.

Very well, you say. But very often we don't know what the "national average" is, or we don't know what the standard deviation of the heights of all college students is, or we don't deal with the kinds of data that lend themselves to measuring means meaningfully. What do we do then? Ah yes, that we shall also come to shortly.

# PRACTICE SHEETS

1. A television commercial states, "Abacin, when tested against the leading brand of plain aspirin, was unsurpassed in the suppression of headaches in men." Assuming that this statement is reporting the results of an experiment, what was the hypothesis that was tested? What do the results indicate? How could the experiment be forced to come up with "significant" results?

2. Currently, the mean age of boys served by the Boys' Clubs nationally is 14 years. You think that here in Elmira things are somewhat different regarding the ages of boys served at the Boys' Clubs, and you would like to petition the national office to permit the local Boys' Club to run a program more appropriate to what you think their age really is. You also know that the standard deviation nationally is 6 years. Your director is not very anxious to bother the national office, but will do so, if you can furnish him with enough "proof." Discuss what you would have to consider and what significance level you would use. Then draw a random sample of 50 youngsters. Suppose you came up with an average age of 16 years. What would you conclude? Also, please discuss the dangers of making a Type I and a Type II error. What would be the consequences of each type of error in this particular case?

3. Suppose you are trying to test against the null hypothesis that says that the mean of your sample is not different from a score of 65 (i.e., that the mean, indeed, is 65). Your level of significance is .05. What would you conclude on the basis of the following z-scores?

   a) +.90                f) +1.3

   b) −1.60               g) +2.0

   c) +2.40               h) −1.5

   d) −1.96               i) +3.0

   e) −1.8                j) −2.3

4. The instruction booklet for the BOO test states that this test has been standarized for college freshmen, and that the mean score is 50, with a standard deviation of 15. You draw a random sample of 36 students from OXU, and obtain a mean of 58; your significance level is .01. State your null hypothesis, the alternative hypothesis, and the probability question. Then do the necessary computations. What would you conclude?

5. A recent study by the Council on Social Work Education indicates that the mean age of graduate social work students throughout the country is 33 years, with a standard deviation of 6 years. Your observations in your classes seem to indicate to you that the students at this school are considerably younger, and you decide to do a study to see if this is so.

   a) State the null hypothesis.

   b) State the alternative hypothesis.

   c) What is a Type I error in this case, and what would be its consequences?

d) What is a Type II error, and what would be its consequences?

e) Suppose you would try to convince the Admissions Committee to change its entrance requirements, or mount a special recruitment effort for older students on the basis of your study. What level of significance do you think would be appropriate? Why?

Suppose you did the study, using a random sample of 50 students, and found that their mean age is 31 years.

f) What is the standard error of the mean for all samples of 50?

g) What is the standard score for your sample?

h) What is the probability?

i) On the basis of your answer to e) above, what would you conclude?

6. An agency is interested in determining if there has been an increase in the number of clients referred for psychological testing. It had previously been assumed that no more than 20% of the clients required such referral. Answer questions a) to d) from question 5. above.

e) Suppose that on the basis of this study, you would try to determine whether it might not be better to hire a psychologist who would be on the staff of your agency, rather than referring clients "out." What level of significance would you choose? Why?

Suppose you did the study, using a random sample of 100 clients, and found that 27 had required referral. Please answer questions f) to i) from question 5. above.

7. In planning a new housing project for individuals over 60, the architect's original plans called for an equal number of apartments for couples and for singles. As the buildings are beginning to rise, hundreds of applications pour in. The sponsors of the project now become concerned whether the architect's projection regarding couples and singles is valid. They suspect that more couples than anticipated are applying. The buildings are not yet completed, so changes are still possible, at some additional cost, of course. Answer questions a) to d) from question 5. above.

e) What level of significance would you suggest to the sponsors for a study of applications? Why?

Suppose you did the study, using a random sample of 90 confirmed applications, and found that 55 were from couples, and 35 were from singles. Please answer questions f) to i) from question 5. above.

# CHAPTER 10
# THE t-DISTRIBUTION (no puns, please)

Before we can move on beyond this place of wrath and tears, we shall have to introduce a new concept — *degrees of freedom.* We could, at this point, grow philosophical about how much freedom certain individuals really have in our society; how little freedom anyone really has, when you stop to think of it, etc. But we won't. We shall be the very model of reticence and even taciturnity, and merely stick to the facts.

As to degrees of freedom, you have all encountered this concept before in the real world out there. For example, I am sure that you have had the experience of being told that you can choose any four courses for next year. Sounds like a lot of freedom. But then you are told that one course (at least) must be from group A and one course from group B. That begins to cut down on your "degrees of freedom." By the time the actual class schedule emerges, you might further realize that by insisting upon taking that course in "Armadillo Sexuality," you have further cut down your real freedom, because it is being given at the same hour on the same day as that other favorite of yours, "Modes and Modalities of Therapeutic Interventions on Behalf of Maimed Individuals in Gestalt-Oriented Encounter Groups in Kepichenitz." So, you had to make a choice between the two (I know what I would choose — give me "Armadillo Sexuality" every time); your complete "freedom" certainly diminished rapidly.

Similarly, in statistics, when we are interested in deviations from the mean, for example, you know that the deviations from the mean will always add up to 0. Suppose I now tell you that we have a total of, say, four cases, and you can make up any deviations you like for our four values — complete freedom. What would happen? Well, let's say you pick 5 for the first one, –10 for the second one, and –9 for the third one. The fourth deviation, then, *must* be 14; you have no other choices, because together the 4 deviations must add up to 0. So really, in this example, where $N = 4$, the degrees of freedom were 3, or $N - 1$.

This same relationship holds true when we move to tables. For example, let us look at the following table:

|       | A  | B  | Total |
|-------|----|----|-------|
| y     |    |    | 40    |
| z     |    |    | 60    |
| **Total** | 50 | 50 | 100   |

If I tell you that you can fill in any real numbers you like in the above table — complete freedom — how much freedom do you really have? Well, first of all, I have limited your freedom by including the totals for the rows (y and z) and for the columns (A and B). That still looks like you have four free choices; actually you only have *one*. The very instant that you put any number into any one of the cells, you have lost all freedom. Try it — you'll see. Actually, then, this kind of table, usually called a 2 x 2 table because it has 2 rows and 2 columns, only has one degree of freedom. It follows our notion of having $N - 1$ degrees of freedom, but in tables, the degrees of freedom are always equal to the (number of rows minus 1) times (the number of columns minus 1); or,

$$df = (r-1)\ (k-1)$$

In this formula, df means degrees of freedom, r means the number of rows, and k means the number of columns in a table.

This relationship will always hold true. If you want to play more games like this, entertain and mystify your friends, and even learn something in the process, you might try just one more table.

| | A | B | C | D | Total |
|---|---|---|---|---|---|
| v | | | | | 80 |
| w | | | | | 90 |
| x | | | | | 100 |
| y | | | | | 70 |
| z | | | | | 60 |
| **Total** | 100 | 100 | 100 | 100 | 400 |

How many free choices do you have? It should come out to be a maximum of 12:

$$df = (r-1)\ (k-1) = (5-1)\ (4-1) = 4 \times 3 = 12$$

In other words, out of 20 possible choices, only 12 are actually "free."

Now that you understand this concept of degrees of freedom, just file it away in your head under the d's, and we will get to how it is used any hour now. You might, in the meantime, contemplate upon how much freedom we really have in a variety of life situations, compared to how much freedom we think we have. Yes, Sophenisba, life is tough.

And because life is tough, Sophenisba, one of the things that sometimes happens is that we do not have the standard deviation of the population at hand; in fact, all we have most of the time is some sample information — a sample mean and a sample standard deviation — but no population mean, and no population standard deviation. It is at trying times like these that the t-test comes to the fore and becomes useful. Actually, the t-distribution is similar to the z-distribution (i.e., the normal distribution), and becomes identical with it when the sample size is infinity. With smaller sample sizes, the t-distribution tends to have a sort of lower hump in the middle, and higher tails at the ends than is true of the normal distribution. Therefore, it has a sort of quality all its own, dependent upon the size of the sample. But just as we calculated a z-score for the normal distribution and then looked up its probability, we will now be able to calculate a t-score and then look it up, keeping in mind, however, that the sample size plays an important role. We therefore look up the probability of any t-distribution in reference to its degrees of freedom. Perhaps a little diagram will help. In the magnificent drawing below, we have indicated the distributions of all possible samples of a certain size, and as you can hopefully see, the distributions vary somewhat from our old friend, the normal distribution, depending upon the size of the sample (i.e., the number of degrees of freedom). As the sample size increases, the distribution does become very similar to the normal distribution. Throughout, if you will just think of our little t's as similar to our old, familiar little z's, life will become much simpler. Also, please remember that (as with z-scores) the greater the t-score is, the further it is removed from the mean, and the lower the probability. As previously, larger t's will give us lower probabilities, which will result in a greater tendency to reject the null hypothesis.

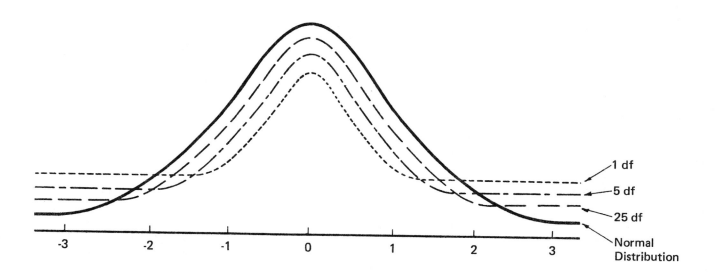

## COMPARISON OF SAMPLE MEAN AND HYPOTHESIZED (POPULATION) MEAN
Let us now see how all this works out with a few cogent examples.

Suppose we want to find out whether our students would score more or less than an average of 86 points on a certain achievement test. We know nothing about *all* students, and we are not going to test *all* of the students — all we will do is take a sample of 16 students and give them the test, and see how they score. Our null hypothesis, then, is that their mean score would be 86. Also, before we actually give them the test, we ought to decide upon our level of significance—at what level will we "believe"? Let us assume we choose the .05 level. We now give the test to the sample of 16 students, and find that their mean score is 80 with a standard deviation of 8. Do we accept our null hypothesis, or what? Note, please, that what we do *not* have is the standard deviation of the original population. What we can do however, is to say that we shall use the standard deviation of our sample to get an estimate of the standard error of the mean:

$$\text{Est. std. error of mean} = \frac{\text{std. dev. of sample}}{\sqrt{n}} = \frac{8}{\sqrt{16}} = \frac{8}{4} = 2$$

$$\text{Then, } t = \frac{\text{sample mean} - \text{hypothesized mean}}{\text{Estd. std. error}} = \frac{80 - 86}{2} = \frac{-6}{2} = -3$$

Our degrees of freedom in such a one-sample case are $n - 1 = 16 - 1 = 15$.

If we now turn to the t-table in the Appendix, we find that firstly, we must look up the degrees of freedom in the left-hand column. Finding 15df, we then look across the row, and find that the t-score for the .05 level for a non-directional hypothesis is 2.13. Since our t-score is even greater than that, we must reject our null hypothesis — our population mean is not 86. In the form of a diagram, this looks as follows:

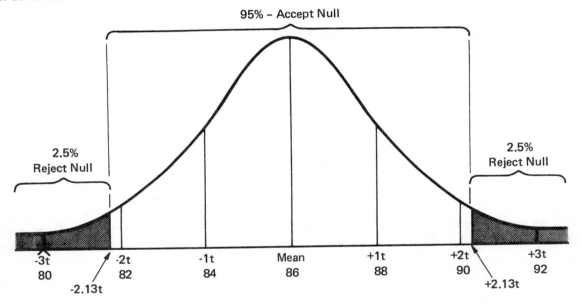

One more example: suppose we thought all along that the mean age of clients served by the ZEX Marriage Counseling Agency is 35 years. Has this changed? To test this we take a random sample of 25 clients, and find that their mean age is 40 years, with a standard deviation of 7 years. Our significance level, since this will involve totally changing the agency's focus, is set at .01. So, what do we do?

$$\text{First, the Est. std. error of mean} = \frac{\text{std. dev. of sample}}{\sqrt{n}} = \frac{7}{\sqrt{25}} = \frac{7}{5} = 1.4$$

$$t = \frac{\text{sample mean} - \text{hyp. mean}}{\text{est. error}} = \frac{40 - 35}{1.4} = \frac{5}{1.4} = 3.57$$

$$df = n - 1 = 25 - 1 = 24$$

If we now look up 24 degrees of freedom, and follow that row to the .01 column for a non-directional test, we find a t-score of 2.80. Since our 3.57 is even greater that that, we conclude that our client population is, indeed, significantly different from 35 years (in this case, older than 35 years).

In a diagram, this looks as follows:

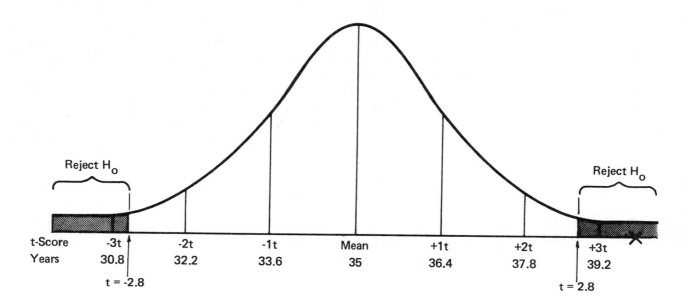

In other words, our sample mean of 40 years is 3.57t above the mean, whereas a t of only 2.8 would have satisfied us.

It might be worthwhile to note two things at this point:

1. Note the importance of the level of significance, and the fact that this should be decided upon before you gather the data. In this case, for example, had we decided upon a significance level of .001, our proof would not have been good enough, because we would have needed a t-score of 3.75 (see table) to reject the $H_o$.

2. Again, note the importance of sample size. Had we done the same study with a sample of only 9, we would have found that the Est. error of mean = $\frac{7}{\sqrt{9}} = \frac{7}{3} = 2.33$. Our value of t would have been $\frac{40 - 35}{2.33} = \frac{5}{2.33} = 2.15$. With that kind of a t-score, and 8 df (9 - 1), we could not have mustered enough proof to reject the $H_o$ at the .01 level (we'd need a t-score of 3.36), and would have concluded that we really can't discard our null hypothesis, and that the mean age of clients of this agency, indeed, is not significantly different from 35 years.

## THE t-TEST AND DIFFERENCES BETWEEN MEANS

Another very handy use of the t-test is when we have the means of two different groups, and we want to compare them to see whether there is a significant difference between them. Our df in such a case = $n_1 + n_2 - 2$; in other words, we lose 1 degree of freedom for each of the samples, and $n_1$ and $n_2$ stand for the sizes of the 2 samples.

Let us take a rather simple example, in which the sample sizes are the same, and in which we can make the assumption that both populations are normally distributed. Let us say that you are working on a study, comparing certain characteristics of the male and female students at your school. You think that there is a difference between the distances that entering male and female students have traveled to school; i.e., more entering female students come from Bali or Singapore, while a greater number of entering male students come from exotic places like Skokie or Canarsie, or the other way around. You decide to test your hypothesis at the .05 level, and draw two random samples of 10 male students and 10 female students. The mean number of miles for your sample of male students is 900 miles, with a std. dev. of 400 miles; for the sample of female students, the mean distance is 750 miles, with a std. dev. of 250 miles. That is:

> Null hypothesis: no difference (mean 1 = mean 2)
> Alternative: mean 1 is not equal to mean 2
> Significance level: .05
> Sample information:
>     Males: M = 900; std. dev. = 400; n = 10
>     Females: M = 750; std. dev. = 250; n = 10
>     $df = n_1 + n_2 - 2 = 10 + 10 - 2 = 20 - 2 = 18$

What we are first interested in here is the (take a deep breath) "estimate of the standard error of the difference between two means." Please, please remember that not long ago we stated that, theoretically, all possible means of a certain size will distribute themselves normally around the true population mean. We will now extend this notion to include the difference between two means, and the testing of a hypothesis regarding the difference between two means. In other words, if two means are really the same (the null hypothesis), then the differences between a large number of samples of these means will distribute themselves also normally, with the mean of these differences being at 0 (no difference), and the other values tending to cluster around this zero difference. Instead of a standard deviation, or an estimated standard error of the mean, we now, in this distribution, speak of an estimated standard error of the difference between means. Once we have calculated that, we will of course go right back to seeing how "far out" the difference that we observed between the two means really is, or , in other words, calculating the probability of obtaining this great a difference between the two means, when, in fact, there is no difference between them (the hull hypothesis). Now, in examples like the above one, where we can assume that both populations are normally distributed but the variances seem to differ (note the s.d. of 400 and 250), the formula for the estimated standard error of the difference between two means is:

$$\text{Est. std. error of diff. between 2 means} = \sqrt{\frac{s_1^2}{n_1} + \frac{s_2^2}{n_2}}$$

In the formula, $s_1$ stands for the standard deviation of the first sample ($n_1$), and $s_2$ stands for the standard deviation of the second sample ($n_2$). You can, of course, use the same formula for samples of different sizes as well. Plugging in our numbers now, we get:

$$\text{Est. std. error of diff.} = \sqrt{\frac{400^2}{10} + \frac{250^2}{10}} = \sqrt{\frac{160,000}{10} + \frac{62,500}{10}}$$

$$= \sqrt{16,000 + 6,250} = \sqrt{22,250} = 149$$

t, then, equals the difference between the two means, divided by the std. error of the diff:

$$t = \frac{900 - 750}{149} = \frac{150}{149} = 1.007 \text{ or } 1.01, \text{ if we want to be charitable.}$$

If we now look at our t-table, along the row of 18 df, we find that t = 2.10 for a non-directional hypothesis at the .05 level. Our t of 1.01 is therefore much too low, and we must conclude that our null hypothesis is correct, and that there seems to be no difference between entering male and female students in terms of the distances they have traveled to school.

In the form of a diagram, this would look as follows:

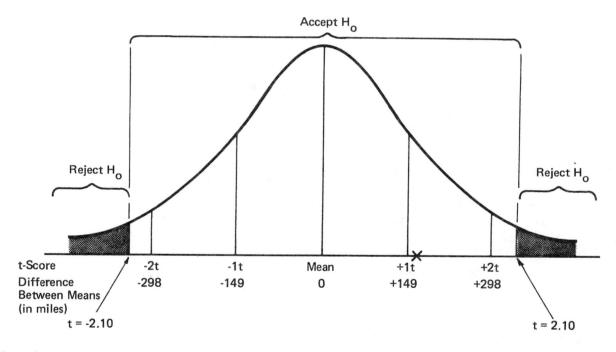

What the above diagram indicates is that under the null hypothesis, all possible differences between the means would distribute themselves in such a way that the mean difference is zero, and that each estimated standard error of the difference between two means equals 149 (i.e., 1t = 149). At the .05 level, with 18 degrees of freedom, we would need a t-score greater than 2.1 in either direction in order to reject the null hypothesis. The t-score we obtained was 1.01, and we therefore are clearly in the region of accepting the null hypothesis.

The above represents the simplest way of approaching t-tests for hypotheses regarding the difference between means. At other times, when, for instance, the sample sizes are very unequal, but the population variances are assumed to be similar, the standard error of the means can be estimated by using a "pooled variance," by which we mean that we have taken the variances (remember, that was the standard deviation squared) and have weighted them by the sample size, arriving at a "pooled variance" (no, we are not going swimming now). The formula for the estimated pooled variance from the data in two samples is:

$$s^2 = \frac{(n_1 - 1) s_1{}^2 + (n_2 - 1) s_2{}^2}{n_1 + n_2 - 2} = \text{it's not as bad as it looks}$$

We then substitute this newly found pooled variance for the squared standard deviations in the formula for the estimated standard error of the difference between the means:

$$\text{Est. std. error of diff. betw. means} = \sqrt{\frac{s^2}{n_1} + \frac{s^2}{n_2}}$$

We can then merrily go along and calculate our t-score, using the same formula we used above, namely:

$$t = \frac{\text{mean}_1 - \text{mean}_2}{\text{Est. std. error of diff. betw. means}}$$

Let us see how this works out, using an example.

This time, I am interested in the difference in heights between adolescent boys and girls at a specific school in the famous township of Pinsk. Having arrived there, I immediately grab a random sample of 17 boys and 10 girls and, upon measuring them from head to toe, find that the mean height of the boys is 64 inches with a standard deviation of 2 inches, while the mean height of the girls is 66 inches with a standard deviation of 3 inches.

Null hypothesis: no significant difference in heights between boys and girls (mean 1 = mean 2).
Alternative: there is a significant difference in heights between boys and girls (mean 1 does not equal mean 2).
Significance level: .05
Sample information:
Boys:  $M_1 = 64$;    $s_1 = 2$;    $n_1 = 17$
Girls:  $M_2 = 66$;    $s_2 = 3$;    $n_2 = 10$
$df = n_1 + n_2 - 2 = 17 + 10 - 2 = 25$

If we now plug this information into our formulas, we get:

$$s^2 = \frac{(n_1 - 1)s_1{}^2 + (n_2 - 1)s_2{}^2}{n_1 + n_2 - 2} = \frac{(16)\,(4) + (9)\,(9)}{25} = 5.8$$

$$\text{Est. std. error of diff.} = \sqrt{\frac{s^2}{n_1} + \frac{s^2}{n_2}} = \sqrt{\frac{5.8}{17} + \frac{5.8}{10}} = \sqrt{.9212} = .96$$

$$t = \frac{\text{Mean}_1 - \text{Mean}_2}{\text{Est. std. error}} = \frac{64-66}{.96} = \frac{-2}{.96} = -2.083$$

Checking the t-table along the row of 25 df, we find that we need a t-value of 2.06 or more (or a −2.06 or less) to reject our null-hypothesis at the .05 level, and accept the non-directional alternative hypothesis. So how did we do? We got a t of −2.083 — just barely over the −2.06 that we needed. We therefore reject the null hypothesis and accept the alternative hypothesis that there is a significant difference in height between these boys and girls. Again, in the form of a diagram, this looks as follows:

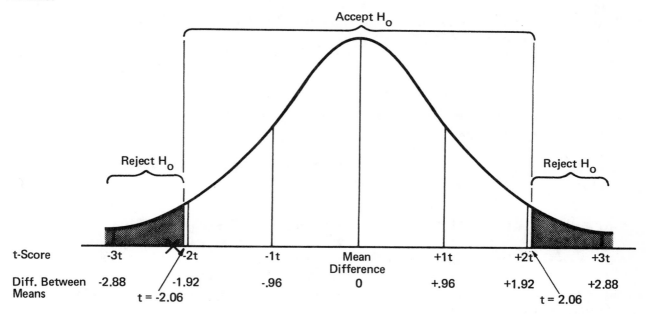

There are numerous other things one can do with t-tests, but we shall refrain from pursuing them. Do, please, note that we have only used t-tests in three ways:

a) to test a hypothesis about a population mean from sample information;

b) to compare two sample means when the sizes of the two samples are similar and/or the population variances are different;

c) to compare two sample means when the sizes of the two samples are not similar and/or the population variances are similar.

Further, please be aware of the fact that, strictly speaking, the t-test is only appropriate if the data meet certain conditions. These are:

a)   the samples must be independent; i.e., the selection of any one case from the population must have no effect upon the selection of any other case;

b)   the populations are theoretically normally distributed;

c)   the variables must be measured at least at an interval level.

You ought to know at this point that there are other tests, even other applications of more complicated t-test formulas, for data that do not meet the above qualifications (independence, for example). Furthermore, the t-test has proven itself to be a rather robust little soul, so that some divergence from the above rules is relatively permissible (the normal distribution of the population, for example).

Finally, it should be stressed that the t-test is particularly handy for small samples, for which we would be hard put to justify using a z-test. There is general agreement, even among researchers, that for samples under 30, the t-test must be used in place of the z-test, and for samples between 30 and 60, it would be advisable to do so. Over 60, it matters less and less, and, by the time you reach infinity, t is normally distributed as z.

## TO SUMMARIZE:

*Use the z-test* when you have large samples (at least 30, and preferably over 60), and when you know the population standard deviation.

*Use the t-test* when you have small samples, when you do not know the population standard deviation, or when you are comparing two sample means.

## A BRIEF NOTE ON ONE-TAILED VERSUS TWO-TAILED TESTS OF HYPOTHESES

Before we go any further, I want you to note the extreme controls which I have exerted throughout this chapter. We have spoken of t-tests (a superb opportunity for all kinds of magnificent puns), then spoke of entering male and entering female students, and now are going to discuss one-tailed vs. two-tailed tests. Through all of this, I have made no jokes, no puns, no allusions to anything which might cause the least bit of disapproval from the D.A.R., the League of Decency, or the San Diego Union. I hope you appreciate the excruciating effort this has taken.

Now then, on to one-tailed vs. two-tailed tests. When we were dealing with z-tests and directional hypotheses, we were dealing with a one-tailed test. In other words, we were saying that our hypothesis was that A indeed is better than B. If we were willing to take a 5 percent chance of being wrong (i.e., a 5 percent chance of making a Type I error), we needed a z-score of 1.64 or more to reject the null hypothesis and accept the directional alternative hypothesis (check Table 1 again). Our diagram, then, of the probability that a z-score of 1.64 would be exceeded, looked as follows:

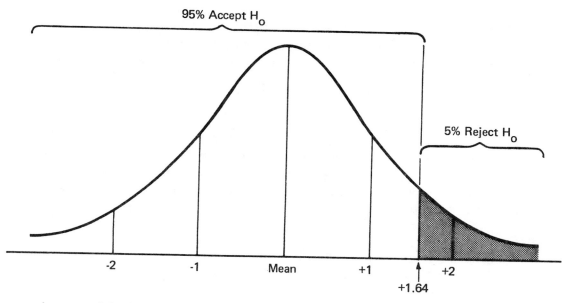

All we are interested in here is that one tail, which is in the direction of our hypothesis. Certainly, if our data had turned out so that A was worse than B, we would not even have bothered doing any tests.

When we have a non-directional hypothesis, however, saying merely that there is a difference between A and B, we are willing to reject the null hypothesis if this difference proves significant in *either* direction. This, at first glance, seems most unfair when compared to directional hypotheses, and indeed something shall have to be done about this. What is done about it, very simply, is to say that if we are still only willing to take a 5 percent chance of making a Type I error, we are going to have to split that 5 percent into the two tails, allowing each tail only 2.5 percent. Thus, again using z-scores and dear old Table 1, we find that our regions for accepting or rejecting the null hypothesis in this case look as follows:

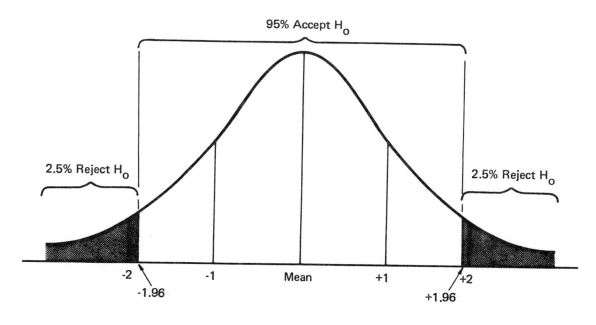

On the basis of this reasoning, then, when we are dealing with a directional hypothesis at a .05 significance level, we can actually use all of that .05 in the tail towards which our directional hypothesis lies. If, on the other hand, we have a non-directional hypothesis and the same significance level of .05, we have to split that .05 into the two tails, resulting in .025 in each tail. In both cases, of course, there are .95 for which we would accept the null hypothesis.

Perhaps an example using the t-test will help. Suppose you wish to examine the effect of sleeplessness upon reaction time. You draw two random samples of 15 students each, and keep one group awake for 48 consecutive hours, while the other group is permitted to follow its normal sleeping patterns. Following the 48 hours, you give both groups a test, measuring their reaction time to the ringing of ancient Chinese gongs. The results are:

Sleepless group: mean = .20 sec.; std. dev. = .04 sec.; n = 15
Slept group: mean = .165 sec.; std. dev. = .03 sec.; n = 15

Our null hypothesis is that there is no difference between the two groups in terms of reaction time. But what is our alternative hypothesis? If it is non-directional, merely stating that there is a difference between the two groups, and our significance level is .01, then we will proceed as follows:

$$\text{Est. std. error of diff.} = \sqrt{\frac{s_1^2}{n_1} + \frac{s_2^2}{n_2}} = \sqrt{\frac{.04^2}{15} + \frac{.03^2}{15}} =$$

$$\sqrt{\frac{.0016}{15} + \frac{.0009}{15}} = \sqrt{\frac{.0025}{15}} = \sqrt{.000166} = .013$$

$$t = \frac{M_1 - M_2}{\text{std. error}} = \frac{.20 - .165}{.013} = \frac{.035}{.013} = 2.69$$

If we now look this up on our t-table, we find that for 28 df (15 + 15 − 2), for a non-directional hypothesis, at the .01 level, our t-score would have to be 2.76. So we did not quite make it in terms of a two-tailed test. This is also illustrated in the diagram on the next page.

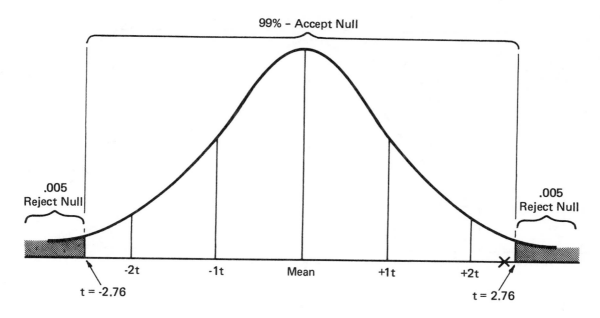

99% – Accept Null

.005
Reject Null

.005
Reject Null

-2t          -1t          Mean          +1t          +2t

t = -2.76                                    t = 2.76

Our t-score of 2.69 is indicated by the X on the above diagram. Please note that with a non-directional hypothesis, and a significance level of .01, we are really splitting this 1 percent into the two tails (1/2 percent, per tail). Our score of 2.69 falls within the "accept null hypothesis" range, and we must, therefore, conclude that we do not have sufficient proof to state that sleeplessness has any effect (positively or negatively) upon reaction time to the ringing of ancient Chinese gongs.

But what if we had done the same experiment, but this time had stated a directional hypothesis: the sleepless group *will* have a significantly slower reaction time than the slept group, when ancient Chinese gongs are rung at them. The significance level would still be .01. What would happen? Firstly, I would obviously not do any calculations at all if the data indicate the opposite direction of my hypothesis; i.e., if the slept group reacted more slowly than the sleepless group, I'd just give up right then and there. So, I'm really only interested if the difference is in the direction in which my hypothesis lies. The mathematics involved would be exactly the same, and I would emerge with the result that t = 2.69. But now, if I look this up on the same table, I have to look along the heading "Probabilities for directional (one-tailed) tests." Now, for 28 df, for a directional hypothesis, and the .01 level, the t-score has to be 2.47. Again, let's look at the following diagram.

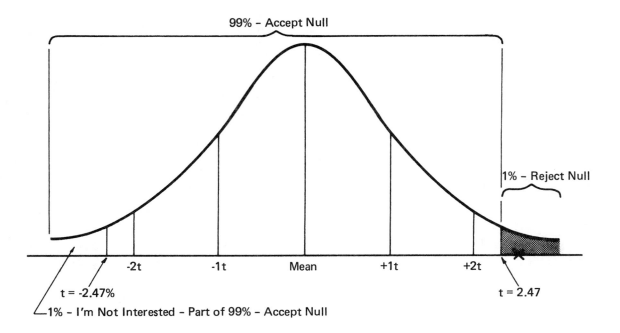

99% – Accept Null

1% – Reject Null

-2t   -1t   Mean   +1t   +2t

t = -2.47%

t = 2.47

1% – I'm Not Interested – Part of 99% – Accept Null

Again, we have indicated our t-score of 2.69 by an X. This time, we see that it falls within the range in which we would reject the null hypothesis and accept the alternative — the reaction time of the sleepless group is indeed longer than the reaction time of the slept group.

In this book, the table of the t-distribution can be used for both one-tailed and two-tailed tests (i.e., for directional and non-directional hypotheses). All you have to do is look along the appropriate row, and then down the appropriate column. Frequently, however, tables only give you the figures for either directional or non-directional hypotheses; Table 1 of the probabilities that a certain z-score will be exceeded, for example, was a table for directional hypotheses only. But by now, you may be aware that if we just play some games around doubling or halving the probabilities, we should be able to use any table for both directional and non-directional hypotheses. And, indeed, this is true. The way it works out is as follows:

If you have a two-tailed table and a non-directional hypothesis, it's O.K. to use the table as is; if you have a two-tailed table and a directional hypothesis, you can double your significance level, and look it up that way. Conversely, if you have a one-tailed table and a directional hypothesis, you're O.K.; if you have a one-tailed table and a non-directional hypothesis, you must cut your significance level in half. Since statistic texts are no more consistent than anything else in life, it pays to read the title of a table before you go plunging into it tail first.

Maybe the following chart will help explain this further.

| Hypothesis | One-tailed table | Two-tailed table |
|---|---|---|
| Directional | O.K. | look up under *double* your significance level |
| Non-directional | look up under *half* of your significance level | O.K. |

We shall not go into this any more deeply, but this little formulation may one day be very helpful unto you. So cut it out, frame it, and for a nominal fee (or even for an ordinal or interval fee) I will be glad to autograph it for your children.

## ON TO CHI-SQUARE!

# PRACTICE SHEETS

1.  You believe that the average age of the children taking part in the Bloodline Program is 13 years. You wish to test that notion, and your significance level is set at .05. Your sample consists of 15 youngsters, and the raw data look as follows:

    9, 11, 10, 13, 17, 4, 3, 7, 16, 8, 15, 8, 6, 12, 11 years

    On the basis of this information, please indicate the following:

    a)  Null hypothesis.

    b)  Alternative hypothesis (non-directional).

    c)  n = ?

    d)  df = ?

    e)  Sample mean = ?

    f)  Sample standard deviation = ?

    g)  Estimated standard error of the mean = ?

    h)  t = ?

    i)  Your decision at .05 level.

    j)  Draw a diagram to illustrate your answers.

2.  In my two statistics classes, I recently made the grave error of giving an exam. The grades on the exam were as follows:

    Class A:  97, 92, 88, 86, 85, 79, 52, 65, 76, 70
    Class B:  58, 71, 60, 98, 86, 90, 84, 40, 83, 70

    I showed these grades to Dr. Goldworth, and he said that these two classes were really different. I told him that I didn't think so. We decided that the .05 level of significance would satisfy us, and thereupon tested the null hypothesis. What were our answers to the following:
    (Note: some of the answers are filled in for you.)

    a)  Null hypothesis.

    b)  Alternative (non-directional).

    c)  n = ?

    d)  df = ?

    e)  Class A mean = 79

    f)  Class B mean = 74

    g)  Class A standard deviation = 13.6

    h)  Class B standard deviation = 17.6

    i)  Estimated standard error of the diff. between means = ?

    j)  t = ?

    k)  Your conclusion at .05 level.

    l)  Draw a diagram to illustrate your answers.

3. Suppose that in the example above Dr. Goldworth had not only insisted that the two classes were different, but had gone on in his inimitable style to insist that Class A was definitely better than Class B. In that case, please state:

   a) Null hypothesis.

   b) Alternative.

   Suppose we had again agreed upon a .05 significance level. All the calculations you did in problem 2 above would remain the same for c) to j). But,

   k) Your conclusion at the .05 level:

   l) Draw a diagram to illustrate your answers.

4. The next time around, I again showed by class grades to Dr. Goldworth. I had already figured the means and standard deviations of the two classes. They were:

   Class A: mean = 86; s.d. = 12; n = 10
   Class B: mean = 75; s.d. = 15; n = 10

   "This time," said Dr. Goldworth, "I'm really sure that these groups are different." So, we tested them again at the .05 level.

   a) Null hypothesis:

   b) Alternative:

   c) n = ?

   d) df = ?

   e) Est. std. error of diff. between means = ?

   f) t = ?

   g) Your conclusion at .05 level:

   h) Draw a diagram to illustrate your answers.

5. What if Dr. Goldworth had insisted again that Class A was definitely the better one?

   a) Null hypothesis:

   b) Alternative:

   Suppose we had again agreed upon a .05 level. All the calculations you did in problem 4 above would remain the same for c) to f). But,

   g) Your conclusion at the .05 level:

   h) Draw a diagram to illustrate your answers.

6. Doing a study of suicide, you wish to test the hypothesis that men, on the average, commit suicide at a younger age than women. From records that are available to you, you draw a random sample of 19 male suicides and 7 female suicides. For the men, the mean age is 45 years, with a standard deviation of 20 years; for the women, the mean age is 48 years and the standard deviation is 18 years. Using the formula for the pooled variance, what is the standard error of the difference between these means? What is the t-score? What is the probability? What do you conclude at the .05 level?

7. You think your neighborhood is beginning to lose those individuals who are becoming more affluent, while replacing them with families whose income is not expanding as rapidly. Using real estate transaction records, you investigate a random sample of 15 families who have moved out during the past 6 months, and find that their mean increase in income over the past 3 years has been $10,000, with a standard deviation of $4,000. You also locate a random sample of 7 families who have recently moved into the neighborhood, and find that their increase in income over the past 3 years has been $7,000, with a standard deviation of $3,000. Using the formula for the pooled variance, what is the standard error of the difference between these means? What is the t-score? What is the probability? What do you conclude at the .10 level?

# CHAPTER 11
# THE CHI-SQUARE(D) DISTRIBUTION

Considerable controversy rages throughout the world of researchers, statisticians, and Maori midgets as to whether the correct name for this next distribution is "chi-square" or "chi-squared." We, with our usual reticence, will not enter into this controversy, except to say that it is totally beyond our understanding why, for all these years, no one has been able to successfully cross-breed an albino rat with a striped mongoose; not that this has anything to do with chi-square, but I felt that now was a good opportunity to get this off my chest.

Now, then: chi-square stands for the Greek letter Chi ($X$), squared.

As you may have noticed — those of you who are still somewhat awake — we did talk about nominal and ordinal variables at the beginning of this book, but soon left them in order to concentrate more fully on interval variables. The question arises, however, as to what we can do with nominal and ordinal data, especially in the social sciences, where so many of the data are of that nature, and where sometimes, in our attempts to quantify all data, we go to such unjustified extremes that we actually may be destroying much of the validity of our data through these manipulations. (Boy, that was a long question!) It is precisely for these kinds of "qualitative" data that the $X^2$ analysis comes in handy.

Conceptually, I hope that it is clear that when we have nominal data, the whole set of statistics dealing with means, medians, standard deviations, and all tests based upon these measurements are useless, and we, therefore, have to find other ways of dealing with such data. The underlying concepts and theories which become useful here are those of pure probability and randomness. Translated into more mundane concepts, we end up with the notion of what is expected according to probability theory, as compared to what is observed. At its simplest, we say that when there is a great difference between what is expected and what is observed, then we are surprised, and think that maybe something other than chance is operating. When, on the other hand, the observed data are close to what we expect, we are not impressed.

And indeed, all $X^2$ really represents is a measure of the difference between what is expected and what is observed. There are some little games which we will play with this notion, but the basic concept remains the same.

## CHI-SQUARE FOR A SINGLE VARIABLE
Let us start with a simple example. Suppose that a researcher is conducting a study of political affiliation among the residents of Kotzen. On the basis of previous studies, he expects the proportions to be:

Republicans — 60 percent; Democrats — 35 percent; Independents — 5 percent

He then does a study of 100 random individuals, and finds that his respondents are:

Republicans — 50 percent; Democrats — 40 percent; Independents — 10 percent

Is the difference between the expected and the observed frequencies significant at, say, the .05 level? Let us set up the data in the form of a table.

## POLITICAL AFFILIATION

|  | Republican | Democrat | Independent | Total |
|---|---|---|---|---|
| Observed (O) | 50 | 40 | 10 | 100 |
| Expected (E) | 60 | 35 | 5 | 100 |

We know by now, going way back to our concepts of deviation, that if we just try to get the differences between the observed and the expected (O - E), we will always end up with zero. So, as usual, we will square the differences. And this time, to get some kind of ratio of difference, we will divide the squared differences by the expected values, and then add the results all together. In the above example, this means:

a) for Republicans: $\dfrac{(O - E)^2}{E} = \dfrac{(50 - 60)^2}{60} = \dfrac{-10^2}{60} = \dfrac{100}{60} = 1.67$

b) for Democrats: $\dfrac{(O - E)^2}{E} = \dfrac{(40 - 35)^2}{35} = \dfrac{5^2}{35} = \dfrac{25}{35} = .71$

c) for Independents: $\dfrac{(O - E)^2}{E} = \dfrac{(10 - 5)^2}{5} = \dfrac{5^2}{5} = \dfrac{25}{5} = \underline{5.00}$

$$\text{Total} = \Sigma \dfrac{(O - E)^2}{E} \quad \dotfill \quad 7.38$$

Thus, $X^2$ for this frequency distribution is 7.38. But what does this mean? For that, we are going to have to plug in some other material first:

a) You remember, no doubt, the concept of degrees of freedom; just as with t-tests, we are dealing with a distribution that is very much influenced by the degrees of freedom. In this particular case, we have three different categories that we are dealing with, and thus we have two degrees of freedom (n - 1). It is important that in looking at $X^2$ we realize that we are dealing with the following question: what is the hypothetical, or theoretical, or probabilistic distribution of the observed numbers among several *categories,* or within the several *cells* of a table? In computing degrees of freedom for $X^2$, then, we are not interested in the sample size as we were with t-tests, but rather in the number of categories or cells, minus one, of course; in the example above, that would be 3 - 1 = 2 df.

b) $X^2$ is a funny distribution — it is not at all normal, but very skewed; also, since it is squared, it can not be a negative number. Usually, we talk of measuring the "goodness of fit" between the observed and the expected, and it is, therefore, impossible to talk of one or two-tailed tests; all $X^2$ tables are nondirectional. It is only by inspection of the data that some direction can sometimes be ascertained. All that the $X^2$ value tells us is what the probability is that these numbers would have distributed themselves as they did by chance.

Just to show you how skewed the distribution of $X^2$ really is, and how important the degrees of freedom are, the following diagram deserves some attention.

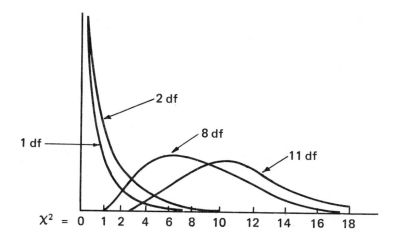

c) We usually speak of "Observed — Expected," but since we then square that number anyway, we always end up with a positive number, and you might just as well say "Expected — Observed." It may be simpler, mathematically, to always subtract the smaller number from the larger one.

d) Note that $X^2$ values are cumulative; i.e., we add them up. Each cell contributes to our total value of $X^2$, and what this means is that we can see just how much each cell difference contributed to our total $X^2$. In the above example, out of a total $X^2$ of 7.38, the Democrats contributed the least (.71), the Republicans contributed 1.67, and it was the Independents who contributed 5.00 to our total value of $X^2$. This indicates, of course, that the largest difference between the Expected and the Observed values was in regard to the Independents.

e) Once we have $X^2$, we can look up the probability of obtaining the results we did obtain on a Table of $X^2$, just as we did with a t-test.

Now that you understand all that, let's go back to our example. We had found that $X^2 = 7.38$. If we now go to our Table of $X^2$ in the Appendix, and look along the row marked 2 df, we find that the value of $X^2$ necessary for a .05 level is 5.99. Since our $X^2$ is 7.38, we did even better than that, and must, therefore, discard the null hypothesis and accept the alternative hypothesis, which says that the political affiliation among Kotzen residents is *not* 60 percent Republican, 35 percent Democrat, and 5 percent Independent. Please note that we cannot say just what the political affiliation of Kotzenians really is — all we can say is that it is not what we expected it to be, taking a 5 percent chance of making a Type I error. We can, however, note that the biggest difference is in the case of the Independents.

One other example of using $X^2$ with a single variable might help. Working in a child guidance clinic, you want to test the hypothesis that this agency serves approximately the same number of children in each age group between 8 and 16 years. Your significance level is .10, and you decide to draw a sample of 80 children. If you divided the ages into four equal intervals, you would expect to get 20 youngsters in each category. Your findings are as follows:

### AGE GROUP

| | 8 - 9 yrs. | 10 - 11 yrs. | 12 - 13 yrs. | 14 - 15 yrs. | Total |
|---|---|---|---|---|---|
| Observed (O) | 19 | 18 | 23 | 20 | 80 |
| Expected (E) | 20 | 20 | 20 | 20 | 80 |

Doing exactly as we did before, we would say that $X^2 = \Sigma \frac{(O - E)^2}{E}$ , or, in this case,

$$X^2 = \frac{(19-20)^2}{20} + \frac{(18-20)^2}{20} + \frac{(23-20)^2}{20} + \frac{(20-20)^2}{20} =$$

$$\frac{1}{20} + \frac{4}{20} + \frac{9}{20} + 0 = \frac{14}{20} = .7$$

Since we here have four categories, we are dealing with three degrees of freedom. If we now look up the $X^2$ value for the .10 level under 3 df, we find that $X^2 = 6.25$. Since our calculated $X^2$ was only .7, we accept the null hypothesis, and conclude that any fluctuations between age groups were just due to chance, and were not significant at the .10 level.

## CHI-SQUARE FOR A 2 X 2 TABLE

Very frequently we deal with a comparison of two or more variables, one or several of which may be nominal or ordinal. We may be interested, for example, to see how well a certain treatment works on an experimental group, as compared to a control group; or whether there is a relationship between political conservativism and marital infidelity; or whether younger therapists tend to become more actively involved with clients than do middle-aged therapists; etc. In these kinds of cases, where we really want to know whether two variables are independent of each other, $X^2$ analyses are also used. You have already learned the basic underlying principle behind $X^2$ analysis — the notion of observed and expected frequencies — and that principle remains the same. Since its application does become somewhat cumbersome in larger tables, or when we are dealing with numbers that are not whole numbers, we will resort to some formulas, which will simplify matters further.

Let us say that we hypothesize that sex among undergraduate students is related to . . . what? Just think of the possibilities . . . All right, back to $X^2$. (Some day, we'll write that other book.) SO — let's try again: suppose we hypothesize that sex among undergraduate students (I mean gender, of course) is related to whether or not the student is currently taking a statistics course. Our significance level is .10. We take a random sample of 100 students, and find the following results:

| | Taking a stat course | Not taking a stat course | Totals |
|---|---|---|---|
| Male | 18 | 37 | 55 |
| Female | 7 | 38 | 45 |
| Totals | 25 | 75 | 100 |

Now, what does this table mean? Well, we do have more males than females taking the stat course; but, on the other hand, there are more males than females in our sample of 100 to start with. Also, for both males and females, more students are not taking a stat course than are — but the females are ahead by only one. It is impossible really to do anything with this table just by looking at it. We shall have to resort to a $X^2$ analysis. Now, we could go back to what we had said previously, and find the expected values for each of the cells, but this would get rather complicated and cumbersome. For example, to find the expected value for "males taking a stat course", we would have to say that of our total of 100 students, 25 or 25/100 took a stat course. If there were no difference between males and females in terms of taking a stat course, then we would expect that 25/100 of our males and 25/100 of our females ought to be taking that course. Thus, the expected value for "males taking a stat course" would be 25/100 of 55, which is 13.75; the expected value for "females taking a stat course" would be 25/100 x 45 = 11.25; etc. I hope you realize that this could get to be very clumsy; especially if we then moved on to take the difference between the Observed and the Expected, square it, and divide by the Expected. Again, for "males taking a stat course" that would mean: $(18 - 13.75)^2/13.75$, and you would have to do this for each and every cell in the table. And that ain't all — since we are approximating a discrete distribution by a continuous one (whatever the hell that means), we would have to introduce a correction factor of $-.5$ into the numerator of each of these fractions before squaring them. That's too much — I quit!

But wait, there is hope yet: although the analysis could be done this cumbersome way, there is a simpler formula. All 2 x 2 tables are set up as follows (we've put letters in place of numbers):

| | Success | Failure | Totals |
|---|---|---|---|
| Group I | a | b | $n_1$ |
| Group II | c | d | $n_2$ |
| Totals | $n_3$ | $n_4$ | N |

In this form, the "small n's" represent the various sub-totals, and the "big N" represents the grand total. All you have to do now is cross-multiply a x d and b x c, subtract the smaller from the larger, square the result, and multiply by N. Then, divide it all by the product of the little n's. Just one more thing — we have to introduce that little correction factor, which here is N divided by 2, and which is called Yates' Correction for Continuity. Putting it all together now, the formula looks as follows:

$$\chi^2 = \frac{\left[\left|ad-bc\right| - \frac{N}{2}\right]^2 N}{(n_1)(n_2)(n_3)(n_4)}$$

In this formula, $|ad-bc|$ indicates the absolute value; i.e., always subtract the smaller from the larger, so you'll get a positive result.

Let us now repeat our table on sex and the statistics course, and put the letters alongside the numbers for easy illustration:

|  | Taking a stat course | Not taking a stat course | Totals |
|---|---|---|---|
| **Male** | 18 (a) | 37 (b) | 55 ($n_1$) |
| **Female** | 7 (c) | 38 (d) | 45 ($n_2$) |
| **Totals** | 25 ($n_3$) | 75 ($n_4$) | 100 (N) |

Plugging this into the formula we now get:

$$\chi^2 = \frac{\left[|(18 \times 38) - (37 \times 7)| - \frac{100}{2}\right]^2 100}{(55)(45)(25)(75)} = \frac{(684-259-50)^2 \ 100}{4,640,625}$$

$$= \frac{(375)^2 \ 100}{4,640,625} = \frac{14,062,500}{4,640,625} = 3.03$$

In case the mathematics involved have frightened you too much, please note that we did this example the most drawn-out way possible. Usually, of course, we would separate the $375^2$, cancel between the numerator and the denominator, and never end up with such a horrendous fraction. Also, of course, it does not matter which of the "little n's" you multiply by which first, or what name you call them, as long as you multiply them all by each other.

Back to our problem: the $\chi^2$ value we obtained was 3.03. Now, what does that mean? First of all, we have to remember that with a 2 x 2 table we have one degree of freedom. (Remember: in the previous chapter we discussed that the number of degrees of freedom for tables = $(r - 1)(k - 1)$. If we now look along the row of 1 df on the $\chi^2$ table, we find that the $\chi^2$ value for .10 is 2.71. Since our $\chi^2$ of 3.03 is greater than that, we conclude that the probability of this happening by chance is less than .10 ($p < .10$), and that there *is* a relationship between the sex of undergraduate students and whether or not they take a statistics course, being willing to take a 10 percent chance of making a Type I error. Please note again that if, on the basis of our findings, we were going to totally restructure the entire research and statistics department of the school, we would have demanded much better proof (say a .01 level), and our data would *not* have given us sufficient proof ($\chi^2 = 6.64$ at .01 with 1 df).

Let's take another example of a 2 x 2 table. Suppose an agency was interested in determining whether clients who are self-referred are more likely to be "continuers" than clients who were referred by another agency. A .05 significance level is chosen, and the study is carried out with 90 clients. Of these

90 clients, 30 were "continuers," and 15 of these were referred by another agency. Of the 60 "non-continuers," 18 were referred by another agency. What is the probability of this occurring by chance, and what can we conclude on the basis of these data if our significance level is .05?

Setting up the data in the form of a table, we get:

|  | Continuers | Non-continuers | Totals |
|---|---|---|---|
| Referrals | 15 | 18 | 33 |
| Non-Referrals | 15 | 42 | 57 |
| Totals | 30 | 60 | 90 |

(You may have noticed that some of the values in the table above had to be deduced from the information we did have.)

Our formula is:

$$\chi^2 = \frac{\left[\left|ad - bc\right| - \dfrac{N}{2}\right]^2 N}{(n_1)(n_2)(n_3)(n_4)} = \frac{\left[\left|(15 \times 42) - (18 \times 15)\right| - \dfrac{90}{2}\right]^2 90}{(33)(57)(30)(60)} = \frac{(630 - 270 - 45)^2\, 90}{(33)(57)(30)(60)}$$

$$= \frac{(315)^2\, 90}{(33)(57)(30)(60)} = \frac{(315)\,\cancel{(315)}\,\overset{7}{\cancel{(90)}}}{\underset{11\quad 19\quad 1\quad 4}{\cancel{(33)}\,\cancel{(57)}\,\cancel{(30)}\,\cancel{(60)}}} = \frac{2205}{836} = 2.64$$

Looking up the $\chi^2$ value necessary to give us a probability of .05 for 1 df, we find 3.84. Since our $\chi^2$ value of 2.64 is less than that, we cannot accept the alternative, and have to conclude that referrals do not seem to have any relationship to continuity.

We hope that the above clarifies the use of $\chi^2$ for 2 x 2 tables, and that you are now ready to move on to bigger and better tables.

## CHI-SQUARE FOR TABLES GREATER THAN 2 X 2

Let us say that we are interested in determining if there is a relationship between age and commitment to ecology (i.e., whether these two variables are independent of each other). We take a random sample of 100 individuals, divide them into "younger" (under 30 years) and "older" (30 years and over), and ask them how strongly committed they feel to doing something about ecology. The results are tabulated as follows:

119

|  | Younger | Older | Total |
|---|---|---|---|
| Very committed | 25 | 25 | 50 |
| Somewhat committed | 10 | 13 | 23 |
| Uncommitted | 5 | 22 | 27 |
| **Total** | 40 | 60 | 100 |

To calculate the $X^2$ value of a table greater than 2 x 2, it is advisable to take the following steps:

a)  Going down one column at a time, take each cell figure, square it, and divide by the row total; add for each column:

For "Younger":  $\dfrac{25^2}{50} + \dfrac{10^2}{23} + \dfrac{5^2}{27} = \dfrac{625}{50} + \dfrac{100}{23} + \dfrac{25}{27} = 12.5 + 4.35 + .93 = 17.78$

For "Older":  $\dfrac{25^2}{50} + \dfrac{13^2}{23} + \dfrac{22^2}{27} = \dfrac{625}{50} + \dfrac{169}{23} + \dfrac{484}{27} = 12.5 + 7.35 + 17.93 = 37.78$

b)  Take each of these answers and divide them by the appropriate column totals:

Younger:  $\dfrac{17.78}{40} = .4445$

Older:  $\dfrac{37.78}{60} = .6297$

c)  Add these and subtract 1:

.4445 + .6297 − 1 = 1.0742 − 1 = .0742

d)  Multiply by N:

.0742 x 100 = 7.42, and that's our $X^2$.

All that now remains is to decide how many degrees of freedom we have. As you undoubtedly remember, df = (r − 1) (k − 1), which here would = 2. Suppose our significance level is .05. Looking up the $X^2$ value for 2 df and a probability of .05, we find it to be 5.99. Since our $X^2$ of 7.42 is greater than that, we conclude that the probability of attaining this result by chance is less than .05 ($p < .05$), and we therefore accept the hypothesis that commitment to ecology is related to age. From inspection of the table, we then further conclude that the direction in which this happens is that younger individuals have a greater tendency to be committed to ecology than do older individuals.

The same kind of analysis and calculations can be carried out for tables of any size, keeping in mind of course, that the degrees of freedom will change.

If you would like to know the mathematical formula for what we have done, it is:

$$\chi^2 = N \left[ \Sigma \, \Sigma \, \frac{x^2}{(x_i)\,(x_j)} - 1 \right]$$

In this formula, x stands for any number in a given cell; $x_i$ stands for the row totals; $x_j$ stands for the column totals; and the rest means what is usually means.

## CAUTIONS REGARDING THE USE OF $\chi^2$

Since $\chi^2$ is such a seductive little tool (believe it or not), there are times when it tends to be inappropriately used. A few words of caution might, therefore, be in order:

a)   The observations which give rise to the data *must be independent* of each other and arise from random samples. That is, they must really be such that one cannot influence the other. For example, in a study of height of college basketball players as related to year of college, one could not make this a continuous study over four years, because your 7 foot freshman might still be in there as a 7 foot sophmore; in fact, by that time, he might be 7'2'' — but he certainly would not have shrunk to less than his original 7 feet.

b)   It is a generally accepted rule that no more than 20 percent of the *expected* frequencies may be less than 5. This means that in rather large tables, where you may have as many as 20 cells (in a 5 x 4 table, for example), you must make sure that you have sufficiently large samples so that no more than 20 percent of the cells have an expected frequency of less than 5, or else you have to collapse some of the categories.

Otherwise, good luck!

# PRACTICE SHEETS

1.  Some theorists maintain that services should be provided in accordance with the number of percentage of any ethnic group within the total population. Others maintain that services ought to be provided on the basis of need, and therefore, if one ethnic group needs more services, then it ought to receive more services. Be that as it may, you hypothesize that in the Model Cities area, services are not being distributed in accordance with the ethnic distribution of the residents of the area. The ethnic composition of the area is approximately as follows:

    Black: 50 percent
    Chicano: 24 percent
    White: 20 percent
    Asian-American: 6 percent

    A study of social services delivered to residents indicates the following percentage distribution:

    Black: 57 percent
    Chicano: 18 percent
    White: 24 percent
    Asian-American: 1 percent

    How would you test your hypothesis? At what significance level? Perform the calculations, and draw a conclusion.

2.  In an experimental study of one-to-one therapy versus group therapy, 60 cases are randomly assigned, and then judged as to how satisfactorily they progressed during a period of three months. The results are as follows:

    |            | Satisfactory | Unsatisfactory | Total |
    |------------|--------------|----------------|-------|
    | One-to-one | 15           | 15             | 30    |
    | Group      | 20           | 10             | 30    |
    | Total      | 35           | 25             | 60    |

    Analyze these data in terms of the following: null and alternative hypotheses; the probability question; significance level; and consequences of Type I and Type II errors. Calculate $X^2$. What do you conclude?

3.  Following this study (in 2. above), somebody else comes along, and says that really, the best results would be obtained by a combination of one-to-one and group therapy. Anxious to do its job as effectively as possible, the agency adds an additional random sample of 40 clients to the study above, and provides them with both one-to-one and group therapy. These cases end up with 30 being judged "satisfactory," and 10 judged as "unsatisfactory" in their progress. Repeat all you did for question 2 above, including the new data.

4. Some researchers are particularly interested in the relationship between father-absence and school drop-outs. They therefore decide to study a random sample of 100 drop-outs during a particular year in a school system, and 100 children of the same age and sex who did not drop out of school.

a) What is the null hypothesis?

b) What is the alternative hypothesis?

c) Suppose the study indicates that 25 of the 100 drop-outs had no father currently in the home, and 12 of the 100 students still in school also had no father in the home. Present these results in an appropriate table.

d) Compute $X^2$ for these data.

e) What is the probability?

f) What would you conclude at the .05 level?

5. In a particular community, there had been very little use of the Community Mental Health Center. A massive one-month informational campaign was undertaken, using speakers, fliers, TV spots, etc. In order to measure the effectiveness of this campaign upon family attitudes toward the Center, a random number of families was interviewed before the campaign, immediately after the compaign, and 6 months later. The attitudes were categorized into "favorable," "neutral," and "unfavorable."

a) What is the null hypothesis?

b) What is the alternative hypothesis?

c) What is a Type I error in this case, and what would be its consequences?

d) What is a Type II error in this case, and what would be its consequences?

Suppose that the level of significance decided upon is .01. The study is then carried out with the following results: of the 50 families interviewed prior to the campaign, 20 were favorable, 10 were neutral, and 20 were unfavorable; of the 60 families interviewed immediately after the campaign, 40 were favorable, 10 were neutral, and 10 were unfavorable; finally, of the 70 families interviewed in the follow-up study 6 months later, 20 were favorable, 30 were neutral, and 20 were unfavorable.

e) Set up an appropriate table to present the results of this study.

f) Compute $X^2$ for these data.

g) What is the probability?

h) What would you conclude at the .01 level?

i) What would you recommend to the Board of Directors of this Mental Health Center?

# CHAPTER 12
# CORRELATION

There are times when we are primarily interested in the way two or more variables "co-relate"; i.e., is there some relationship between what happens to one variable and what happens to the other; or, do these two variables vary together, and if so, to what extent? Please note that we are not speaking of *causal* relationships here. Two variables can certainly co-relate, or correlate, without there being a cause and effect relationship between them. Thus, for example, there is usually a considerably high correlation between the height and weight of children — that is, taller children tend to weigh more than shorter children, or heavier children tend to be taller than skinnier kids. But it would be impossible, on the basis of a correlation analysis, to say that increased weight causes increased height, or that increased height causes increased weight. In fact, of course, both height and weight may be caused by a combination of other factors, such as heredity, nutrition, etc. We can, and often do find all kinds of spurious relationships between two variables, which just happen to change in tandem, so to speak, but which are really totally unrelated to each other. Thus, for example, during recent years, there has been a considerable increase in the number of so-called pornographic establishments in the downtown areas of major cities in our country, as well as an increase in the salaries of clergymen. I sincerely hope and pray that the correlation between these two variables is not due to any real relationship between them.

Keeping all this stuff about clergymen and pornography in mind, let us now turn to, first, a logical approach to correlation; then we'll go on to learning how to measure it.

If you have a job which pays you on an hourly basis at the rate of $4.00 per hour, then I hope it is clear that there is a relationship between the variable "hours worked" and the variable "money earned" (for the sake of our illustration, please don't bother me with income tax deductions, social security, or with the fact that you lie on your timesheet). In fact, the relationship is a perfect, straight-line correlation — for every hour worked, you get $4.00. This relationship is illustrated in Graph 12.1

Obviously, as the graph indicates, for 2 hours of work, you get $8.00; for 5 hours of work, you get $20.00; etc. This, then, is a perfect, or exact positive correlation.

Let us suppose, however, that you only have a maximum of 20 hours available; you realize that every hour you work is going to mean one hour less devoted to hedonistic pursuits (what else?). Now here we have the opposite relationship of the one we had between money and hours worked. This time, instead of the variable "money earned" going up (or down) step in step with the variable "hours worked," your "hedonism hours" are going to go down as the working hours go up, and go up as the working hours go down. This relationship is illustrated in Graph 12.2.

# Graph 12.1

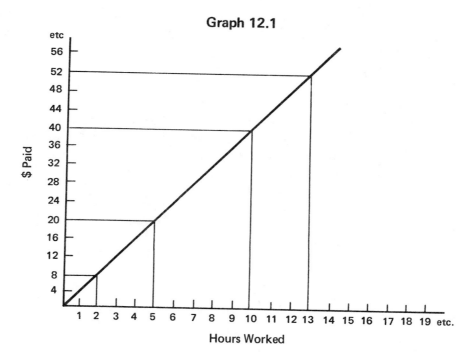

Hours Worked

# Graph 12.2

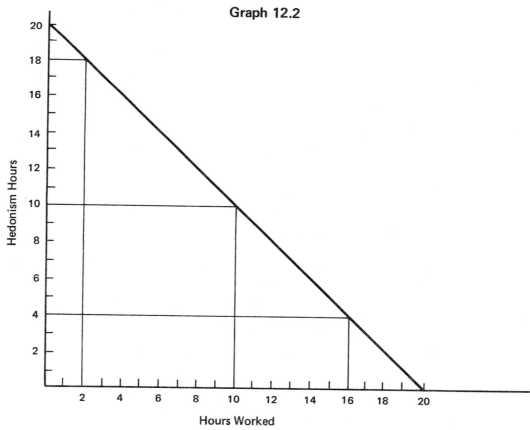

Hours Worked

You can see clearly now that if you are only going to work 2 hours, you'll still have 18 hours left during which to hedonize; working 10 hours is going to cut fun-time down to 10 hours, and working 16 hours — well, it hardly pays to live anymore. What we have here, then, is a perfect negative correlation.

Of course, most relationships between variables (as between people) are not perfect, and when we try to plot them on a graph, we do not end up with such simple straight lines, containing all the points on the graph. Let's take another example — and just to show how deeply committed I am to the Protestant Work Ethic, this one too will deal with putting you to work. Let us assume that this time you have taken a job where there is no hourly rate of pay at all — you are only getting commission on the items you sell. Now what can we expect? Well, clearly, if you are not there at all, you don't make any sales, and therefore earn no money; there may be days when you just come in for a few hours, but make several big sales; at other times, you may work a 12-hour day, but you just can't convince anyone to buy diamond-studded flea collars. Suppose you take the first ten days you've worked under this new arrangement, and graph the relationship between "hours worked" and "money earned."

**Graph 12.3**

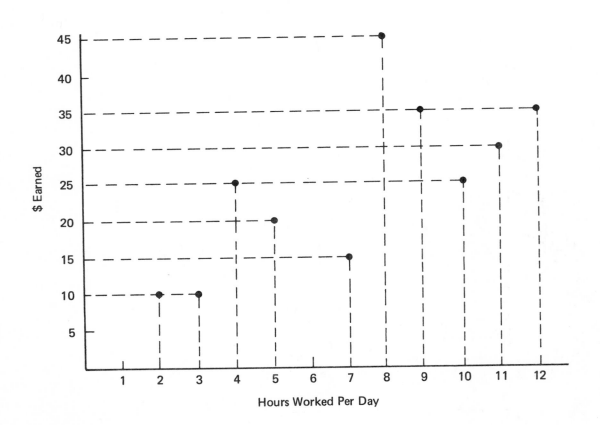

126

Looking at this graph, it becomes clear that although there does seem to be a general trend in terms of the relationship between the two variables, it is certainly not as consistent and simple as it was in the first graph of this chapter. Thus, for example, there was one day when you worked only 4 hours, but earned $25.00; another time when 8 hours of work resulted in $45.00; but then, again, there was a 7 hour day during which you only earned $15.00; and that long, hard 10-hour day, when you made the same $25.00 you had earned that previous 4-hour day. What we have here is a more complex relationship between two variables, which can be measured by means of a correlation analysis.

## PEARSON'S PRODUCT-MOMENT CORRELATION

We could go on for considerable length, plotting more and more graphs to illustrate more and more relationships between two variables. But enough! I think I made my point: two variables can correlate with each other positively (when one goes up, the other does too; when one goes down, so does the other); or negatively (when one goes up, the other goes down); or, of course, not at all (they just have no relationship). I am sure you have guessed by now that here, too, we have some statistical ways of expressing the degree of relationship between two variables. Probably the most important of these is what is known as Pearson's Product Moment Correlation Co-efficient, usually abbreviated, thank God, to Pearson's r, or better yet, just r. Pearson's r can range from $-1$, which is a perfectly negative correlation (Graph 12.2), to $+1$, which is a perfectly positive correlation (Graph 12.1); no correlation at all would end up with a Pearson's r of 0. Thus, if we say that two variables have an r of .60, this indicates a fair positive correlation; if they have an r of $-.65$, this indicates a moderate negative correlation.

Let us now calculate r from the data on Graph 12.3, calling the number of hours worked X, and the money earned Y, and set up the data in several columns: X, Y, $X^2$, $Y^2$, and XY; then we will add each of these columns. This looks as follows:

| Day | X | Y | $X^2$ | $Y^2$ | XY |
|---|---|---|---|---|---|
| A | 2 | 10 | 4 | 100 | 20 |
| B | 3 | 10 | 9 | 100 | 30 |
| C | 4 | 25 | 16 | 625 | 100 |
| D | 5 | 20 | 25 | 400 | 100 |
| E | 7 | 15 | 49 | 225 | 105 |
| F | 8 | 45 | 64 | 2025 | 360 |
| G | 9 | 35 | 81 | 1225 | 315 |
| H | 10 | 25 | 100 | 625 | 250 |
| I | 11 | 30 | 121 | 900 | 330 |
| J | 12 | 35 | 144 | 1225 | 420 |
| N = 10 | $\Sigma X = 71$ | $\Sigma Y = 250$ | $\Sigma X^2 = 613$ | $\Sigma Y^2 = 7450$ | $\Sigma XY = 2030$ |

Now let's just make sure we know what all of these crazy numbers mean: X = the number of hours worked, and Y = the amount of money earned on that day; $X^2$ = the number of hours squared, $Y^2$ = the money earned squared, and XY = the product of X and Y. We then added all these columns.

The formula for r itself looks rather formidable, but after what you've been through so far in this book, it should not unduly disturb your composure.

$$r = \frac{N(\Sigma XY) - (\Sigma X)(\Sigma Y)}{\sqrt{[N(\Sigma X^2) - (\Sigma X)^2][N(\Sigma Y^2) - (\Sigma Y)^2]}}$$

Substituting the appropriate numbers, we get:

$$r = \frac{10(2030) - (71)(250)}{\sqrt{[10(613) - (71)^2][10(7450) - (250)^2]}} = \frac{2{,}550}{\sqrt{(1089)(12{,}000)}}$$

$$= \frac{2{,}550}{\sqrt{13{,}068{,}000}} = \frac{2{,}550}{3{,}615} = .705$$

So, after all this, what do we have? Well, we know that r is positive, and that means that the correlation is a positive one. Furthermore, it is .705, which seems to be moderately high. Yes, but how high is high? We can answer this question, actually, in two ways. First, we can go back to what we have been doing in these past few chapters, and test the hypothesis of whether there is a significant correlation between hours worked and money earned at, say, the .05 level of significance. There are several ways of doing this, but probably the simplest is to convert our r to a t- or z-score. You remember, undoubtedly, that the general rule of thumb says that if we are dealing with an N of less than 30, we must use the t-test; with an N of 30-60 it is still advisable to do so; and with an N of over 60, we can certainly use the z-scores. In the above example, we had a total of 10 days of work, so N = 10. We will use the following formula to transform our r to t:

$$t = r\sqrt{\frac{N-2}{1-r^2}} = .705\sqrt{\frac{10-2}{1-(.705)^2}} = .705\sqrt{\frac{8}{1-.497}}$$

$$= .705\sqrt{\frac{8}{.503}} = .705\sqrt{15.90} = .705(3.99) = 2.813$$

The degrees of freedom, since we are dealing with 2 variables and 2 columns of data, equal N-2, or, in this case, 8. If we now look up the t-score needed for a non-directional hypothesis at the .05 level for 8 df, we find it to be 2.31. With our t-score of 2.81, we can therefore reject the null hypothesis and conclude that our correlation of .705 was significant at the .05 level.

If our sample size had been greater than 30 (and certainly if it had been greater than 60), we could have used a z-transformation instead of the t-transformation. Let us assume that we had that same correlation of .705, but this time with an N of 50. We could now say:

$$z = r\sqrt{N-1} = .705\sqrt{50-1} = .705\sqrt{49} = .705(7) = 4.935$$

If we look up this z-score, we don't find it — it's that far out. We do know that a z-score of 4.0 corresponds to a p of .00003. Even doubling this, as we would have to with a non-directional hypothesis, we end up way beyond our .05 level.

What we have established thus far, then, is that we have a positive correlation, moderately high (.705), which is significant at the .05 level. But still, we would like to know more. What is the extent of the correlation between these two variables? What does that .705 really indicate? This leads us to the second way of interpreting and dealing with r.

If you look back at that rather complicated formula for r, there may be some parts that look suspiciously familiar — all those sums of $X^2$ and $Y^2$ and XY. And, indeed, what the formula actually accomplishes is to calculate a standard score for each of the scores under X and Y, then cross-multiply them, add the products of this cross-multiplication, and divide by N to give us a mean of these cross-products. Pearson's calling this the "product moment correlation" had nothing to do with time; in his day, statisticians used the terms "moment" and "mean" interchangeably, and he was thus talking about a product-mean correlation. What r tells us, then, is the extent to which, on the average, one variable changes in relation to a one-unit standard score change in the other. In our case, then, this would mean that for every 1.0 standard score change in hours worked, there is a .705 standard score change in money earned, and vice versa. But we rarely walk around thinking in terms of relative standard score changes. It is more useful, at this point, to remember that the square of our standard deviation (way back in Chapter 6) was the variance. If we square our r value, what we obtain is a measure of how much of the variation in one variable is accounted for by the other. Thus, if we just take our r of .705 and square it, we get $r^2 = .497$. What this means, then, is that almost 50 percent of the variance in money earned is explained by hours worked. That is noteworthy, and easier to understand conceptually as well. We know that in most situations there are several variables involved which have an impact upon the outcome at which we are looking. In this case, besides the number of hours worked, there may be the number of customers; the number of other salespersons; the relative prices of products in your store, as compared to other stores in the neighborhood; plus, perhaps, ten other variables, all of which play some role in determining the outcome of "money earned." What we do know now, however, is that the single variable "hours worked" accounts for approximately 50 percent of the variations in the amount of money earned. We also know, simultaneously, that there is another 50 percent of variance in money earned, which was not explained by the hours worked, and must therefore be due to the impact of some of these other variables. There are methods of dealing with "multiple correlation analyses," but they are regrettably beyond the scope of this book.

It should also be pointed out that r and $r^2$ are appropriate only to the measurement of a *linear* (i.e., rectilinear) relationship between two variables; i.e., their relationship can be plotted on a graph in a straight line. Note that many relationships between variables are not linear, but rather curvaceous (take strength and age, or income and age, for example). If you have some doubts as to whether or not your data are representing a linear relationship, plot them out on a graph first, and see what this "scatter diagram" looks like. Note the examples that follow:

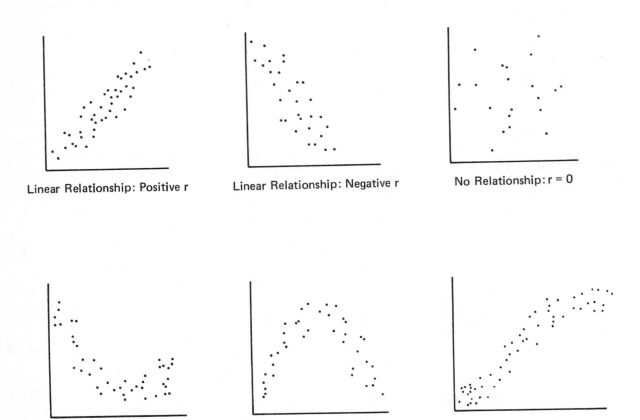

Linear Relationship: Positive r  Linear Relationship: Negative r  No Relationship: r = 0

Curvilinear Relationships – Do **Not** Use r.

## SPEARMAN'S RANK ORDER CORRELATION

There are times when the data we have are in the form of ranks, or where it might make sense to rank the data we have obtained. In such cases, we use a test called the Spearman Rank Order Correlation, which results in a statistic called rho, and which is similar to Pearson's r in the way it is interpreted. For example, suppose we are interested in the correlation between students' scores on the GRE and their last year's grade point average (GPA). We therefore pull out the records of a random sample of 15 students, and for each student we note his or her GPA and GRE. We then rank how each student did on these tests, in comparison to the other students. Thus, the student with the highest GPA score is ranked 1, the next highest score is ranked 2, etc. We will then calculate the differences between ranks, square the differences, and add them up. In a table, this looks as follows:

| Student | GPA Rank | GRE Rank | d | $d^2$ |
|---------|----------|----------|-----|-------|
| A | 1 | 2 | −1 | 1 |
| B | 2 | 3 | −1 | 1 |
| C | 3 | 6 | −3 | 9 |
| D | 4 | 7 | −3 | 9 |
| E | 5 | 1 | 4 | 16 |
| F | 6 | 4 | 2 | 4 |
| G | 7 | 5 | 2 | 4 |
| H | 8 | 10 | −2 | 4 |
| I | 9 | 11 | −2 | 4 |
| J | 10 | 8 | 2 | 4 |
| K | 11 | 9 | 2 | 4 |
| L | 12 | 12 | 0 | 0 |
| M | 13 | 15 | −2 | 4 |
| N | 14 | 13 | 1 | 1 |
| O | 15 | 14 | 1 | 1 |

N=15 $\qquad\qquad\qquad\qquad\qquad\qquad\qquad\qquad$ $\Sigma d^2 = 66$

Then, rho $= 1 - \dfrac{6\Sigma d^2}{N(N^2-1)}$

That "6" is a magic number and is always used in computing rho.

$$= 1 - \frac{6(66)}{15(225-1)}$$

$$= 1 - \frac{396}{3360}$$

$$= 1 - .118$$

$$= .882$$

In other words, the correlation between GPA and GRE ranks for these 15 students is approximately +.88.

As we did with Pearson's r, we can now take the rho of .88, and interpret it. First of all, we see that there is generally a rather high, positive correlation between GPA and GRE. Squaring the rho of .88 results in .774, indicating that approximately 77% of the variance of GPA is explained by the GRE ranks, and vice versa. Furthermore, we can again transform our rho to a t-score by saying:

$$t = \text{rho}\sqrt{\frac{N-2}{1-\text{rho}^2}} = .88\sqrt{\frac{15-2}{1-(.88)^2}} = .88\sqrt{\frac{13}{1-.774}}$$

$$= .88\sqrt{\frac{13}{.226}} = .88\sqrt{57.5} = .88(7.58)$$

$$= 6.67$$

In the case of this correlation, if we were testing the directional hypothesis that GPA and GRE are positively related to each other, we would now look up a t of 6.67, with 13 degrees of freedom (N-2). The table indicates that with a directional hypothesis, a t of 4.22 corresponds to a probability of less than .0005. We would thus certainly conclude that the correlation we found was significant even at the .001 level, and beyond.

Again, had we been dealing with a larger sample (an N of 50 or 60, for example), we could have used the same z-transformation as we did with Pearson's r; namely, $z = \text{rho} \sqrt{N - 1}$.

One last, final, ultimate note on Spearman's Rank Order Correlation. Occasionally, two or more individuals may have the same score for a specific variable, and should, therefore, end up with the same rank. Simultaneously, however, a group of 10 ranked subjects (or scores) should end up with ranks from 1 to 10. What we do, then, is give to each of the tied ranks the average of the ranks that would have been assigned, if there had been no ties. What this means in English is that if, for example, two scores are tied for second place, each of them receives the rank of 2.5 (the average of 2 and 3), and the next score is then ranked in fourth place. This procedure is not only valid for Spearman's rho, but is the usual procedure whenever we deal with tied ranks.

## RELIABILITY TESTING

It is worth noting that correlational analyses are also very useful in establishing the reliability of instruments to be used in research. Thus, the same test could be given to the same group twice, and the correlation between the two scores calculated by means of a Pearson's r. Here again, you have a reliable instrument, if the test-retest correlation is high (preferably .70, .80 or more). Another way of testing the reliability of some instruments is through the use of the split-halves method, whereby the instrument is administered to a group of subjects only once, but the items are then randomly split into two equal groups. Pearson's r can then be calculated using the pairs of scores. In this case, however, since the final instrument will be twice as large as each of the two halves you are testing against each other, you have to "correct" the r you obtained by using the following formula:

$$r \text{ (corrected)} = \frac{2r \text{ (uncorrected)}}{1 + r \text{ (uncorrected)}}$$

Thus, for example, if you had performed a split-half reliability test on your little instrument and had found that r = .51, you would "correct" this by:

$$r = \frac{2(.51)}{1 + .51} = \frac{1.02}{1.51} = .675$$

So you've managed to boost your r of .51 up to .675; but face it, that's still not anything to get ecstatic about — your instrument is not very reliable. Of course, the standards that we use here are more stringent than those used when we are just trying to determine whether a relationship exists between two variables. In constructing test instruments, we want the instrument to be as reliable as possible — our research is going to have to depend on it.

## CONCLUSION

I hope that the above gave you, generally, a brief introduction to the area of correlation, and familiarity with some of the basic ways of employing correlation as a tool in statistical analysis. Again, I want to point out that there are other ways of dealing with the relationship between two variables, including exotic "tests" such as Kendall's tau, correlation ratios (eta), point-biserial, partial, and multiple correlations, regression measures, analyses of covariance, and above all, Applebroog's Hetero-Homo- and Bisexual Concordance for Clustering Variables Suffering from Homoscedasticity. Some of these, and other exciting topics, can be found in more advanced books.

In very general terms, we might summarize the relative meaning of the values of the correlation coefficient as follows:

0 - .20 negligible correlation
.20 - .40 low correlation
.40 - .60 moderate correlation
.60 - .80 considerable correlation
.80 - 1.00 high correlation

There are times when we try to summarize the correlations between several variables in one table, and this is then called a Correlation Matrix. You can always recognize one by the fact that it looks only half filled out, and/or has a whole series of 1.00's running diagonally through it. For example, the correlations done between several variables measured by means of scales in a recent study of a sample of the elderly, could be presented as follows:

|  | Mobility | Gen. Ment. Health | Anxiety | Depression | Delusion | Isolation | Phys. Health |
|---|---|---|---|---|---|---|---|
| **Mobility** | 1.00 | .42 | .30 | .42 | .17 | .11 | .37 |
| **Gen. M.H.** |  | 1.00 | .76 | .80 | .44 | .39 | .89 |
| **Anxiety** |  |  | 1.00 | .49 | .37 | .20 | .54 |
| **Depression** |  |  |  | 1.00 | .32 | .41 | .59 |
| **Delusion** |  |  |  |  | 1.00 | .22 | .36 |
| **Isolation** |  |  |  |  |  | 1.00 | .26 |
| **Phys. Health** |  |  |  |  |  |  | 1.00 |

In this kind of matrix, there is no need to fill in the lower left half of the table, because it would just be a mirror image of the upper right half. What the table indicates, for example, is that the correlation between depression and physical health is .59, between depression and general mental health is .80, etc. — all of which is rather depressing. Usually, this kind of table also has all kinds of asterisks or other kinds of fancy doo-dads next to some of the correlations to indicate their level of significance. By now, you really ought to be able to look at such tables without feeling green all over — try it, you'll even understand it.

# PRACTICE SHEETS

1.  a)  List five pairs of variables that you think have a high positive correlation.

    b)  List five pairs of variables that you think have a moderate positive correlation.

    c)  List five that you think have no or only little correlation.

    d)  List five that you think have a moderate negative correlation.

    e)  And, finally, list five that you think have a high negative correlation.

2.  The following is a listing of a random sample of 10 major cities in Mexico, together with their average January and August temperature and rainfall.

| City | Temperature Jan. | Temperature Aug. | Rainfall Jan. | Rainfall Aug. |
|------|------|------|------|------|
| Acapulco | 78 | 83 | .4 | 9.8 |
| Colima | 72 | 78 | .5 | 7.2 |
| Chihuahua | 49 | 75 | .1 | 3.7 |
| Guadalajara | 58 | 68 | .7 | 7.9 |
| Jalapa | 58 | 66 | 2.1 | 8.0 |
| Merida | 73 | 81 | 1.2 | 5.1 |
| Oaxaca | 63 | 69 | .1 | 4.1 |
| Queretaro | 57 | 67 | .4 | 3.4 |
| Tampico | 65 | 82 | 2.1 | 5.9 |
| Tepic | 63 | 74 | 1.2 | 11.5 |

    a)  Calculate the correlation between the January and August temperatures, and interpret (use r, get the probability, explained variance, etc.)

    b)  Calculate the correlation between January and August rainfall, and interpret (use r).

    c)  Calculate the correlation between the temperature and rainfall in August and interpret (rank the cities and use rho).

3.  A recent study dealt with the relationship between IQ level and self-esteem, as measured on the Narcissus Scale. The results for a sample of 10 students were as follows:

| Student | IQ | Self-esteem | Student | IQ | Self-esteem |
|---------|-----|-------------|---------|-----|-------------|
| A | 100 | 64 | F | 107 | 58 |
| B | 104 | 59 | G | 130 | 76 |
| C | 91 | 67 | H | 136 | 85 |
| D | 128 | 77 | I | 95 | 51 |
| E | 93 | 55 | J | 111 | 71 |

Calculate the correlation (use rho) and interpret your results (probability, explained variance, etc.).

134

4. In a study to determine factors associated with favoritism towards students as displayed by faculty members at any other institution (not here, of course), the researchers asked a teacher to rank 10 of the students in the class according to how well this instructor liked these students. Subsequently, the Verrückter Hauptmann Obedience Scale was administered to the same group of 10 unfortunate students. The results were as follows:

| Student | Teacher Rank | Obediance Score |
|---------|--------------|-----------------|
| A | 1 | 12.1 |
| B | 2 | 13.2 |
| C | 3 | 11.5 |
| D | 4 | 10.5 |
| E | 5 | 10.8 |
| F | 6 | 11.9 |
| G | 7 | 11.3 |
| H | 8 | 10.0 |
| I | 9 | 9.7 |
| J | 10 | 9.2 |

Please analyze and interpret.

5. Usually, professors believe that students who do well in one subject are likely to also do well in other subjects. At our school, however, Prof. Feeley insists that there is a basic difference between students who are "cerebral" and those who "feel deeply"; furthermore, he states that students who do well with clients in the field would do poorly in a "cerebral" subject such as statistics, and vice versa. Prof. Doey disagrees and proposes that in order to test Prof. Feeley's hypothesis, they take a sample of 13 students, have them ranked by their field instructors, and compare these rankings to how they did on their final exam in statistics. The agreed-upon level of significance is .01. The results for the 13 students are as follows:

| Student: | A | B | C | D | E | F | G | H | I | J | K | L | M |
|----------|---|---|---|---|---|---|---|---|---|---|---|---|---|
| Field Rank: | 3 | 5 | 8 | 12 | 2 | 4 | 7 | 11 | 1 | 6 | 13 | 9 | 10 |
| Stat. Final: | 96 | 98 | 77 | 71 | 84 | 90 | 69 | 50 | 87 | 81 | 60 | 64 | 74 |

On the basis of these data, what conclusion would you reach?

6. You have recently developed two instruments to measure the acquiescence level of Cartesian subordinates, and decide that before you run off and actually use them on the unsuspecting, you had better test their reliability first. For one of the instruments, you use a test-retest, while for the other, you divide the test randomly into two parts and use a split-half technique. Below are the results you obtained with your pre-test group of subjects (to make the mathematics easier, we are pretending that you only used 5 subjects for your reliability check):

|   | Instrument I | | Instrument II | |
|---|---|---|---|---|
|   | Test | Re-test | One half | The other half |
| A | 87 | 104 | 25 | 30 |
| B | 47 | 29 | 12 | 3 |
| C | 138 | 152 | 28 | 10 |
| D | 150 | 138 | 21 | 12 |
| E | 110 | 90 | 12 | 14 |

Calculate r and discuss the reliability of your instruments.

7. In a recent study of a sample of aged individuals, the researchers were interested in the correlations between several factors, among them age, health (self-reported), financial well-being, life satisfaction, and anomie. The data for 10 subjects are indicated below. In all instances, the scales have been scored in such a way that high=good; e.g., a financial well-being score of 84 indicates that the subject is better off financially than someone with a score of 62.

| Subject | Age | Health | Financial | Life Sat. | Anomie |
|---|---|---|---|---|---|
| A | 72 | 6.1 | 81 | 3.1 | 9.5 |
| B | 70 | 8.1 | 91 | 4.8 | 17.4 |
| C | 65 | 8.5 | 50 | 2.2 | 10.6 |
| D | 82 | 7.3 | 62 | 4.9 | 16.3 |
| E | 81 | 7.0 | 59 | 3.3 | 11.7 |
| F | 74 | 8.3 | 73 | 3.8 | 15.2 |
| G | 80 | 7.5 | 68 | 3.3 | 12.8 |
| H | 91 | 6.1 | 55 | 4.7 | 14.1 |
| I | 72 | 7.8 | 84 | 4.5 | 13.9 |
| J | 66 | 8.7 | 86 | 4.6 | 18.0 |

Usually, with this kind of study you would use many more subjects and analyze the data using several highly sophisticated methods, with the help of a computer, of course. For our purposes here, please calculate either r or rho, and fill in the following matrix, also indicating the probability of the results you obtained (for calculating the probabilities, pretend that N = 20.). Note that there are 10 different correlations to calculate for the matrix. After you're all finished with the matrix, pray tell, what do the data indicate? Here is the matrix:

|   | Age | Health | Financial | Life Sat. | Anomie |
|---|---|---|---|---|---|
| Age | 1.00 | | | | |
| Health | | 1.00 | | | |
| Financial | | | 1.00 | | |
| Life Satis. | | | | 1.00 | |
| Anomie | | | | | 1.00 |

# CHAPTER 13
# JUST FOR FUN

In this chapter, we shall try to present a few rather simple tests, which may come in handy under certain conditions. They are all based purely upon probability theory, and, therefore, are not subject to some of the requirements (of normal distribution, for example) to which other tests must adhere. These tests, frequently referred to as "non-parametric," really deal with the "order" in which certain data turn up. Spearman's rho and $X^2$ were two such tests — we did not have any notion as to the normal or abnormal distribution of the variable, but merely asked, "What is the probability that the data would distribute themselves as they did, if in reality the null hypothesis is true?" With the tests presented in this chapter, we will be asking ourselves the same question. This really, then, goes back to the notion of a poker game, in which Jesse James gets one - two - three - four - etc. full houses in a row.

Most of these tests (at least all the ones we will be presenting here) are mathematically very simple, and can frequently be used in the place of some of the other tests (z or t tests, for example). Since, however, you really can't get something for nothing, it should be noted that these tests are not as "powerful" as a z or t test. This means that they really require more evidence than the so-called "parametric" tests to give us comparable conclusions. On the other hand, they are so simple, that it sometimes pays to use them instead of a parametric test. If the results are satisfactory, you don't have to go any further; if the results are not satisfactory, you can then try a parametric test to see if your results prove significant with that more powerful statistical tool. On the third hand, of course, there are some instances when only these non-parametric tests are appropriate, and then you cannot use a parametric test.

So, without further ado, let us move on to the three non-parametric techniques in this chapter: the Sign test, the Wilcoxon Signed-Ranks test, and Phi and C Coefficients.

## SIGN TEST

The reason a Sign test is called a Sign test is that this test is only concerned with plus and minus signs, rather than with any mathematical manipulations of the data. It is especially useful when we have pairs of observations of the same individuals or groups of matched individuals; or when we have one observation of pairs of individuals; or when we have different pairs under different conditions. Thus, for example, we could record the data of the test scores of the same individuals before and after a certain lecture was presented; or, we could give two classes of students the same series of weekly quizzes, and after a certain number of weeks see if there was any difference between the classes; or, we could ask two different judges to rate social work students' interventions in a group situation, and determine whether or not these two judges really differ in their ratings. What we need is at least ordinal data, but the Sign test can also be applied to interval data. The underlying theory of the

Sign test rests upon the assumption that if nothing is happening (i.e., the null hypothesis is true), then there is as much chance of positive change (+) as there is of a negative change (−). The question then becomes, really, "What is the probability of getting, for example, 8 pluses out of 10 tries?" And since we already have tables all set up for this type of question, all you have to do is look up the answer. Let us see how this works out with a cement example (I'm getting tired of concrete ones).

One of the main purposes of RELY (the initials stand for Redundancy, Equivocation, Loquacity, and Yechch) is to educate the public regarding the extreme threat of everything to the American Way of Life. Wondering if their message was really getting across, they hired a researcher to give the famous Motherhood-Applepie-Allamerican Patriotism and Chauvinism Test to their audience both before and after their presentation entitled "Why Everything is a Threat to the American Way of Life." At this particular mass rally, 12 people attended. Their scores on the test, both before and after the presentation, and the sign of change is indicated in the table below:

| Individual | "Before" Score | "After" Score | Sign of Difference |
|------------|----------------|---------------|--------------------|
| A | 24 | 26 | + |
| B | 25 | 24 | − |
| C | 34 | 32 | − |
| D | 31 | 28 | − |
| E | 25 | 25 | 0 |
| F | 30 | 26 | − |
| G | 37 | 35 | − |
| H | 19 | 23 | + |
| I | 40 | 38 | − |
| J | 22 | 17 | − |
| K | 32 | 30 | − |
| L | 27 | 20 | − |

In all, then, we had a sample of 12 individuals, 11 of whom showed a change; since ties don't count in a Sign test, we shall have to use N = 11. Of these 11 individuals, 2 showed a positive change, and 9 showed a negative change. Is this significant? I.e., what is the probability of getting these results by chance? Well, all you have to do is look up the probability on Table 4 in the Appendix. There, under N = 11, the probability of getting a sign (either + or −) to appear with a frequency of 2 is indicated as being .033. If your significance level was .10 with a non-directional hypothesis, for example, you would double the .033 to give you .066, and then would reject the null hypothesis and conclude that the presentation made by RELY did indeed have an impact upon this audience — a negative one (from RELY's viewpoint).

All you have to do with a Sign test, then, is list your paired scores or observations, assign a + or − to each pair, discard ties, and look up the probability under the appropriate N and the frequency of the *fewer* sign.

Let us look at another example: suppose that a total of 22 children were asked to rate their understanding of mothers' and fathers' belief in corporal punishment, and that the understanding of mothers' beliefs was greater than that of fathers' beliefs in 12 cases, while the understanding of fathers' beliefs was greater in 6 cases, with 4 ties. Using a sign test, we simply say that our N = 18 (22 minus the 4 ties), and look up the probability under N = 18 and the frequency of the "fewer" sign, which was 6. We then find the probability to be .119 (or, doubled, .238) — hardly significant at all.

When we have an N of more than 25, we can transform the results to a z-score by saying that:

$$z = \frac{\left| \frac{F+}{N} - .50 \right| - \frac{1}{2N}}{\sqrt{\frac{(.50)(.50)}{N}}}$$

In this formula, F+ stands for the frequency of the + sign, and | | again means the absolute value (i.e., always subtract the smaller from the larger). To show you how simple this really is, if we reworked the problem above (even though N is only 18), we would say that:

$$z = \frac{\left| \frac{12}{18} - .50 \right| - \frac{1}{36}}{\sqrt{\frac{(.50)(.50)}{18}}} = \frac{\left| .667 - .50 \right| - .028}{\sqrt{\frac{.25}{18}}} = \frac{.139}{.118} = 1.18$$

If we then look up a z-score of 1.2 (rounding off the 1.18), we find a probability of .115, which, as you can see, is quite close to the probability of .119 which we obtained with our Sign test above.

But really, the Sign test is most useful as a "quickie" for small samples. To give you just one more example: In a recent study, interventions of "socialization" and "treatment" workers were compared along five different dimensions. For each dimension, treatment workers received a higher score, indicating more active intervention; but for each dimension, the difference was so slight that it was not significant. Nevertheless, there was this trend — always in the same direction. By using the Sign test, the researcher was able to determine the fact that the probability of getting this result (i.e., 0 signs in one direction) out of 5 tests was .031. In other words, although each of the individual tests proved non-significant, the Sign test, looking at the over-all pattern, was able to indicate that the results were significant.

## THE WILCOXON SIGNED-RANKS TEST

While the Sign test only takes into account the direction of the differences, this test also gives weight to the amount of difference observed. Again, mathematically, it is very simple: all we have to do is list the scores for the pairs, note the differences in scores, rank these differences, add the positive and negative ranks, and, finally, look up the result of the smaller sum of this addition on Table 5 in the Appendix. In practice, it works out like this:

Suppose we want to see the impact of Dr. Lobis' lecture on anthropoid musicology upon a group of 10 tone-deaf piccolo players, as measured by the Doremifa test. The data are tabulated, the difference between them is indicated in the column marked "d", and these differences are then ranked; i.e., the *smallest* difference is labeled 1, the next to the smallest 2, etc. For our group, this looks as follows:

| Piccolo Player | Before Score | After Score | d | Ranked d's (with sign of d) |
|---|---|---|---|---|
| A | 81 | 97 | 16 | 9 |
| B | 72 | 70 | -2 | -1 |
| C | 57 | 60 | 3 | 2 |
| D | 76 | 82 | 6 | 5.5 |
| E | 75 | 71 | -4 | -3 |
| F | 51 | 61 | 10 | 8 |
| G | 64 | 69 | 5 | 4 |
| H | 66 | 74 | 8 | 7 |
| I | 57 | 63 | 6 | 5.5 |
| J | 69 | 93 | 24 | 10 |

Suppose that we had made the hypothesis that Dr. Lobis' lecture would increase the knowledge of the 10 tone-deaf piccolo players, and had set our significance level at .05.

In the above table, we have two ranks from negative d's (1 and 3). Adding these together, and keeping the sign, we amazingly get -4. On the positive side, however, we have all the other ranks, which together add up to 51. We then take the *smaller* of the two numbers (4) and, with it in hand, consult Table 5. We had a directional hypothesis, and, therefore, are using a one-tailed test. If we now look along the row marked N = 10 (we had 10 subjects), we note that for a one-tailed test a value of 8 would have been significant at the .025 level; a value of 5 would have been significant at the .01 level; and a value of 3 at the .005 level. Our value of 4, therefore, falls somewhere between .01 and .005, certainly better than our significance level. We therefore discard the null hypothesis, and conclude that Dr. Lobis' lecture did have a positive impact upon our 10 subjects.

Please note that in this test, as interpreted in this table, *smaller* values are "better" than *larger* values. This is in direct contrast to what we have been doing in the cases of t-tests and $X^2$, but remember that here we are not dealing with the kind of distribution which measures "distance from the mean", but rather with the question of, "If the null hypothesis is true, how come *so few* of the differences are in one direction?" If, indeed, we do get significantly fewer differences in one direction than we would expect, then we tend to conclude that we should discard our null hypothesis and accept the alternate. The tables for the Sign-test and for the Signed-Ranks Test could, of course, have been set up the opposite way, reflecting the "larger" values; but we like small numbers, so the tables are arranged for us to look up the "fewer."

As with the Sign test, differences of 0 (i.e., tied scores) are dropped from the analysis, and the N is reduced by the number of tied scores.

You might also note that the Wilcoxon Signed-Ranks test is somewhat more powerful than the Sign test. Had we applied a Sign test to the same distribution of piccolo players' scores above, we would have come up with the fact that with an N of 10, we had 2 minus signs. Looking this up on Table 4, we find that the probability is .055. With our original significance level of .05, this would not have been sufficient proof for us to discard the null hypothesis. The Wilcoxon Signed-Ranks test, on the other hand, taking into account not only the direction but also the extent of differences observed, gave us a probability of less than .01, leading us to reject the null hypothesis.

As you have undoubtedly guessed by now, there is a way of transforming the Wilcoxon "scores" to z-scores, when we have an N of more than 25. In such cases, if we call the smaller sum of the ranks "T," then the formula is:

$$z = \frac{T - \frac{N(N+1)}{4}}{\sqrt{\frac{N(N+1)(2N+1)}{24}}}$$

Although in our example we only had an N of 10, let us try out this z-transformation to see how close an approximation we get. In our case, then, N = 10 and T = 4. Plugging these into the formula, we get:

$$z = \frac{4 - \frac{10(10+1)}{4}}{\sqrt{\frac{10(10+1)(20+1)}{24}}} = \frac{4 - \frac{110}{4}}{\sqrt{\frac{(110)(21)}{24}}} = \frac{4 - 27.5}{\sqrt{96.25}} = \frac{-23.5}{9.81} = -2.396$$

Looking up a z of 2.396 (or 2.4), we find that it corresponds to a probability of .008. On the basis of the Wilcoxon Signed-Ranks test, we had concluded that the probability was between .005 and .01. As you can see, the z-transformation works out very well, even with a sample as small as 10, but certainly can be used when you have an N of more than 25.

## PHI ($\phi$) AND C COEFFICIENTS

In Chapter 11, dealing with $X^2$, we worked with the notion that a statistically significant $X^2$ indicated a relationship between the two variables. In Chapter 12, dealing with correlation, we found two measures (r and rho) that indicate **the degree** of relationship between two variables. We were then able to transform that r or rho to a t or z to determine whether this degree of relationship was significant. Conversely, we have some measures which indicate the degree of relationship between two variables, when a $X^2$ analysis has indicated the existence of a significant relationship. These are the Phi Coefficient ($\phi$) for two-by-two tables, and the Contingency Coefficient (C) for tables larger than two by two.

Looking back at Chapter 11, we used as one example the data from a supposed study of the relationship between sex and taking a statistics course. Analyzing the data of that two-by-two table, with an N of 100, we arrived at a $X^2$ of 3.03, which was significant at the .10 level. If we now want to find out the degree of this relationship, we say:

$$\phi = \sqrt{\frac{X^2}{N}} = \sqrt{\frac{3.03}{100}} = \sqrt{.0303} = .174$$

This $\phi$ of .174 can be interpreted similarly to r or rho, except that one should note that obtained by the above method, it is always a positive number, and thus ranges from 0 to +1.0. What we have in the above example, then, is a case where the relationship between the two variables is significant at the .10 level (as indicated by $X^2$), and where the degree of relationship is very slight (as indicated by $\phi$).

When we are dealing with tables larger than two-by-two, we do not use the $\phi$ Coefficient, but use the Contingency Coefficient (C) instead. Again, looking back at the example given in Chapter 11, when we tried to determine whether a relationship existed between age and commitment to ecology, using an N of 100, we arrived at a $X^2$ of 7.42, which was significant at the .05 level. Trying now to determine the degree of this relationship, we say:

$$C = \sqrt{\frac{X^2}{N + X^2}} = \sqrt{\frac{7.42}{100 + 7.42}} = \sqrt{\frac{7.42}{107.42}} = \sqrt{.069} = .263$$

Here, again, C can be interpreted similarly to other correlation coefficients, and on the basis of the above data, we would conclude that there is a significant relationship between the two variables at the .05 level (as indicated by $X^2$), and that the degree of this relationship is slight (as indicated by C).

Our conclusions regarding both $\phi$ and C for the above examples may at first sound somewhat confusing. How can we say that the relationship was *significant* (that sounds like a lot), and then say that the degree of the relationship was only *slight* (that sounds like such a little). To remove confusion regarding this seeming contradiction, let's note a few things: tests of significance, which tell us whether or not a certain relationship (or a certain difference) is statistically significant, merely indicate the probability of the events we're looking at occurring the way they did. Now, certainly, the greater the differences or relations we find, the greater the likelihood that our data are "significant." But also note the importance of sample size — with an N of 10,000, just about any difference will prove to be "statistically significant." It is really, then, another step to ask, "O.K., so the difference or the relationship is significant. But is it noteworthy? Is it important? Is it considerable?" For example, if we compared the heights of college freshmen in two states with samples of 2,000 each, then a 1/4 inch difference in average height would be significant at the .05 level; with samples of 10,000 each, a difference of .09 inches is significant at the .05 level. But are these differences of 1/4 inch or .09 inches noteworthy? Do they *really* make a difference? In most instances I can think of, the answer would be, "No." Thus, it is very well possible to find a relationship which is "significant," but at the same time "slight."

Finally, we ought to say a few words about the limitations of C as a measure of correlation. Since C is derived from $X^2$ by means of the above formula, it can never attain the measure of perfect correlation (i.e., 1). The upper limit of C depends upon the degrees of freedom, and this in itself also means that C values are not totally comparable unless they come from tables of the same size. Obviously, C can not be used with any data for which a $X^2$ would be inappropriate. Finally, although we have said that C is comparable to r or rho, this is not a direct comparability (i.e., r does not equal C). Nevertheless, C is widely used because it does have the advantage of being applicable to data in which the variables are only measured at the nominal level and in which no assumptions can be made regarding the population distribution of the scores.

# PRACTICE SHEETS

1. Prof. Pruzbalovich has 2 statistics classes, to which he gives the same weekly quiz. For the first 7 weeks of the semester, the class averages for the 2 classes have been as follows:

   Monday class:      86, 92, 84, 76, 87, 85, 74
   Wednesday class:   92, 90, 92, 81, 91, 86, 86

   Being of a naturally suspicious nature, Prof. Pruzbalovich is afraid that the Monday class is feeding some of the quiz answers to the Wednesday class. He wonders if the Wednesday class is really doing better than the Monday class, and decides to test this hypothesis at the .05 level.

   a) Do a Sign test to test Prof. Pruzbalovich's hypothesis. What do you conclude?

   b) Do a Wilcoxon Signed-Ranks test on Prof. Pruzbalovich's hypothesis. What do you conclude?

2. It also occurs to Prof. Pruzbalovich that perhaps it's not the cheating — perhaps the Wednesday class just knows the material better — maybe they are brighter, or maybe he lectures better on Wednesdays. He, therefore, decides to continue giving both classes essentially the same quizzes, but with some of the numbers changed for the Wednesday class. The tests are still equivalent, but the correct answers are no longer the same. For the next five weeks, he gets the following results:

   Monday class:      81, 75, 79, 84, 80
   Wednesday class:   86, 75, 82, 80, 82

   a) Taking all 12 quizzes together, what would you conclude on the basis of a Sign test (at the .05 level)?

   b) Would you also do a Wilcoxon Signed-Ranks test? Why?

3. To evaluate a recent pilot training project for the wives of stroke patients, a test was administered to the participants both before and after the training sessions. The scores for the 27 participants were:

| Trainee | Before | After |
|---|---|---|
| 1 | 81 | 78 |
| 2 | 63 | 64 |
| 3 | 85 | 85 |
| 4 | 69 | 73 |
| 5 | 62 | 70 |
| 6 | 86 | 86 |
| 7 | 67 | 70 |
| 8 | 79 | 78 |
| 9 | 88 | 90 |
| 10 | 60 | 67 |
| 11 | 71 | 68 |
| 12 | 85 | 87 |
| 13 | 63 | 67 |
| 14 | 72 | 75 |
| 15 | 94 | 92 |
| 16 | 70 | 74 |
| 17 | 76 | 81 |
| 18 | 97 | 90 |
| 19 | 89 | 96 |
| 20 | 78 | 79 |
| 21 | 91 | 99 |
| 22 | 93 | 95 |
| 23 | 72 | 68 |
| 24 | 94 | 96 |
| 25 | 75 | 81 |
| 26 | 86 | 85 |
| 27 | 88 | 96 |

The hospital administrator wants to make sure that this program really results in greater knowledge on the part of the participants. You have therefore set the level of significance at .01.

a)   Do a Sign test on the above data, as well as a z-transformation. What do you conclude?

b)   Now do a Wilcoxon Signed-Ranks test, and a z-transformation. What do you conclude? (Caution: Watch out for tied ranks.)

4.   Go back to Problem 2 in Chapter 11. What is the degree of relationship between the two variables?

5.   Do the same for Problem 3, Chapter 11.

6.   And Problem 4, Chapter 11.

7.   And, finally, Problem 5 of Chapter 11.

# APPENDIX A
# TABLES

## TABLE 1

### BRIEF TABLE OF THE PROBABILITIES THAT A GIVEN z-SCORE WILL BE EXCEEDED
#### (i.e., what's left in the tail)

| Std. Score (z) | Probability that z will be exceeded |
|:---:|:---:|
| 0.00 | .500 |
| 0.10 | .460 |
| 0.20 | .421 |
| 0.30 | .382 |
| 0.40 | .345 |
| 0.50 | .308 |
| 0.60 | .274 |
| 0.70 | .242 |
| 0.80 | .212 |
| 0.90 | .184 |
| 1.00 | .159 |
| 1.10 | .136 |
| 1.20 | .115 |
| 1.28 | .100 |
| 1.30 | .097 |
| 1.40 | .081 |
| 1.50 | .067 |
| 1.60 | .055 |
| 1.64 | .050 |
| 1.70 | .045 |
| 1.80 | .036 |
| 1.90 | .029 |
| 1.96 | .025 |
| 2.00 | .023 |
| 2.10 | .018 |
| 2.20 | .014 |
| 2.30 | .011 |
| 2.32 | .010 |
| 2.40 | .008 |
| 2.50 | .006 |
| 2.60 | .005 |
| 2.70 | .004 |
| 2.80 | .003 |
| 2.90 | .002 |
| 3.00 | .001 |
| 3.50 | .0002 |
| 4.00 | .00003 |

# TABLE 2

## t-DISTRIBUTION

Probability points of the t-distribution for one and
two-tailed tests of hypotheses.

| | Probabilities for directional (one-tailed) tests | | | | | | | |
|---|---|---|---|---|---|---|---|---|
| | .25 | .10 | .05 | .025 | .01 | .005 | .001 | .0005 |
| | Probabilities for non-directional (two-tailed) tests | | | | | | | |
| df | .50 | .20 | .10 | .05 | .02 | .01 | .002 | .001 |
| 1 | 1.000 | 3.08 | 6.31 | 12.71 | 31.82 | 63.66 | 318.31 | 636.62 |
| 2 | .816 | 1.89 | 2.92 | 4.30 | 6.97 | 9.93 | 22.33 | 31.60 |
| 3 | .765 | 1.64 | 2.35 | 3.18 | 4.54 | 5.84 | 10.21 | 12.92 |
| 4 | .741 | 1.53 | 2.13 | 2.78 | 3.75 | 4.60 | 7.17 | 8.61 |
| 5 | .727 | 1.48 | 2.02 | 2.57 | 3.37 | 4.03 | 5.89 | 6.87 |
| 6 | .718 | 1.44 | 1.94 | 2.45 | 3.14 | 3.71 | 5.21 | 5.96 |
| 7 | .711 | 1.42 | 1.90 | 2.37 | 3.00 | 3.50 | 4.79 | 5.41 |
| 8 | .706 | 1.40 | 1.86 | 2.31 | 2.90 | 3.36 | 4.50 | 5.04 |
| 9 | .703 | 1.38 | 1.83 | 2.26 | 2.82 | 3.25 | 4.30 | 4.78 |
| 10 | .700 | 1.37 | 1.81 | 2.23 | 2.76 | 3.17 | 4.14 | 4.59 |
| 11 | .697 | 1.36 | 1.80 | 2.20 | 2.72 | 3.11 | 4.03 | 4.44 |
| 12 | .695 | 1.36 | 1.78 | 2.18 | 2.68 | 3.06 | 3.93 | 4.32 |
| 13 | .694 | 1.35 | 1.77 | 2.16 | 2.65 | 3.01 | 3.85 | 4.22 |
| 14 | .692 | 1.35 | 1.76 | 2.15 | 2.62 | 2.98 | 3.79 | 4.14 |
| 15 | .691 | 1.34 | 1.75 | 2.13 | 2.60 | 2.95 | 3.73 | 4.07 |
| 16 | .690 | 1.34 | 1.75 | 2.12 | 2.58 | 2.92 | 3.69 | 4.02 |
| 17 | .689 | 1.33 | 1.74 | 2.11 | 2.57 | 2.90 | 3.65 | 3.97 |
| 18 | .688 | 1.33 | 1.73 | 2.10 | 2.55 | 2.88 | 3.61 | 3.92 |
| 19 | .688 | 1.33 | 1.73 | 2.09 | 2.54 | 2.86 | 3.58 | 3.88 |
| 20 | .687 | 1.33 | 1.73 | 2.09 | 2.53 | 2.85 | 3.55 | 3.85 |
| 21 | .686 | 1.32 | 1.72 | 2.08 | 2.52 | 2.83 | 3.53 | 3.82 |
| 22 | .686 | 1.32 | 1.72 | 2.07 | 2.51 | 2.82 | 3.51 | 3.79 |
| 23 | .685 | 1.32 | 1.71 | 2.07 | 2.50 | 2.81 | 3.49 | 3.77 |
| 24 | .685 | 1.32 | 1.71 | 2.06 | 2.49 | 2.80 | 3.47 | 3.75 |
| 25 | .684 | 1.32 | 1.71 | 2.06 | 2.49 | 2.79 | 3.45 | 3.73 |
| 26 | .684 | 1.32 | 1.71 | 2.06 | 2.48 | 2.78 | 3.44 | 3.71 |
| 27 | .684 | 1.31 | 1.70 | 2.05 | 2.47 | 2.77 | 3.42 | 3.69 |
| 28 | .683 | 1.31 | 1.70 | 2.05 | 2.47 | 2.76 | 3.41 | 3.67 |
| 29 | .683 | 1.31 | 1.70 | 2.05 | 2.46 | 2.76 | 3.40 | 3.66 |
| 30 | .683 | 1.31 | 1.70 | 2.04 | 2.46 | 2.75 | 3.39 | 3.65 |
| 40 | .681 | 1.30 | 1.68 | 2.02 | 2.42 | 2.70 | 3.31 | 3.55 |
| 60 | .679 | 1.30 | 1.67 | 2.00 | 2.39 | 2.66 | 3.23 | 3.46 |
| 120 | .677 | 1.29 | 1.66 | 1.98 | 2.36 | 2.62 | 3.16 | 3.37 |
| ∞ | .674 | 1.28 | 1.65 | 1.96 | 2.33 | 2.58 | 3.09 | 3.29 |

# TABLE 3

## CHI-SQUARE DISTRIBUTION

Probability points of the chi-square distribution

| df | Probability values | | | | | | |
|----|------|------|------|------|------|------|------|
| | .30 | .20 | .10 | .05 | .02 | .01 | .001 |
| 1 | 1.07 | 1.64 | 2.71 | 3.84 | 5.41 | 6.64 | 10.83 |
| 2 | 2.41 | 3.22 | 4.60 | 5.99 | 7.82 | 9.21 | 13.82 |
| 3 | 3.66 | 4.64 | 6.25 | 7.82 | 9.84 | 11.34 | 16.27 |
| 4 | 4.88 | 5.99 | 7.78 | 9.49 | 11.67 | 13.28 | 18.46 |
| 5 | 6.06 | 7.29 | 9.24 | 11.07 | 13.39 | 15.09 | 20.52 |
| 6 | 7.23 | 8.56 | 10.64 | 12.59 | 15.03 | 16.81 | 22.46 |
| 7 | 8.38 | 9.80 | 12.02 | 14.07 | 16.62 | 18.48 | 24.32 |
| 8 | 9.52 | 11.03 | 13.36 | 15.51 | 18.17 | 20.09 | 26.12 |
| 9 | 10.66 | 12.24 | 14.68 | 16.92 | 19.68 | 21.67 | 27.88 |
| 10 | 11.78 | 13.44 | 15.99 | 18.31 | 21.16 | 23.21 | 29.59 |
| 11 | 12.90 | 14.63 | 17.28 | 19.68 | 22.62 | 24.72 | 31.26 |
| 12 | 14.01 | 15.81 | 18.55 | 21.03 | 24.05 | 26.22 | 32.91 |
| 13 | 15.12 | 16.98 | 19.81 | 22.36 | 25.47 | 27.69 | 34.53 |
| 14 | 16.22 | 18.15 | 21.06 | 23.68 | 26.87 | 29.14 | 36.12 |
| 15 | 17.32 | 19.31 | 22.31 | 25.00 | 28.26 | 30.58 | 37.70 |
| 16 | 18.42 | 20.46 | 23.54 | 26.30 | 29.63 | 32.00 | 39.25 |
| 17 | 19.51 | 21.62 | 24.77 | 27.59 | 31.00 | 33.41 | 40.79 |
| 18 | 20.60 | 22.76 | 25.99 | 28.87 | 32.35 | 34.80 | 42.31 |
| 19 | 21.69 | 23.90 | 27.20 | 30.14 | 33.69 | 36.19 | 43.82 |
| 20 | 22.78 | 25.04 | 28.41 | 31.41 | 35.02 | 37.57 | 45.32 |
| 21 | 23.86 | 26.17 | 29.62 | 32.67 | 36.34 | 38.93 | 46.80 |
| 22 | 24.94 | 27.30 | 30.81 | 33.92 | 37.66 | 40.29 | 48.27 |
| 23 | 26.02 | 28.43 | 32.01 | 35.17 | 38.97 | 41.64 | 49.73 |
| 24 | 27.10 | 29.55 | 33.20 | 36.42 | 40.27 | 42.98 | 51.18 |
| 25 | 28.17 | 30.68 | 34.38 | 37.65 | 41.57 | 44.31 | 52.62 |
| 26 | 29.25 | 31.80 | 35.56 | 38.88 | 42.86 | 45.64 | 54.05 |
| 27 | 30.32 | 32.91 | 36.74 | 40.11 | 44.14 | 46.96 | 55.48 |
| 28 | 31.39 | 34.03 | 37.92 | 41.34 | 45.42 | 48.28 | 56.89 |
| 29 | 32.46 | 35.14 | 39.09 | 42.56 | 46.69 | 49.59 | 58.30 |
| 30 | 33.53 | 36.25 | 40.26 | 43.77 | 47.96 | 50.89 | 59.70 |

Adapted from P. Games and G. Klare, *Elementary Statistics,* New York: McGraw-Hill, 1961.

# TABLE 4

## DISTRIBUTION FOR THE SIGN TEST

Probabilities indicated below are for one-tailed tests;
for two-tailed tests, double the probability.

| N = | 3 | | N = | 11 | | N = | 17 | | N = | 23 |
|---|---|---|---|---|---|---|---|---|---|---|
| O | .125 | | O | .000 | | 2 | .001 | | 4 | .001 |
| | | | 1 | .006 | | 3 | .006 | | 5 | .005 |
| N = | 4 | | 2 | .033 | | 4 | .025 | | 6 | .017 |
| O | .062 | | 3 | .113 | | 5 | .072 | | 7 | .047 |
| 1 | .312 | | 4 | .274 | | 6 | .166 | | 8 | .105 |
| | | | | | | | | | 9 | .202 |
| N = | 5 | | N = | 12 | | N = | 18 | | | |
| O | .031 | | 1 | .003 | | 3 | .004 | | N = | 24 |
| 1 | .188 | | 2 | .019 | | 4 | .015 | | 5 | .003 |
| | | | 3 | .073 | | 5 | .048 | | 6 | .011 |
| N = | 6 | | 4 | .194 | | 6 | .119 | | 7 | .032 |
| O | .016 | | | | | 7 | .240 | | 8 | .076 |
| 1 | .109 | | N = | 13 | | | | | 9 | .154 |
| 2 | .344 | | 1 | .002 | | N = | 19 | | | |
| | | | 2 | .011 | | 3 | .002 | | N = | 25 |
| N = | 7 | | 3 | .046 | | 4 | .010 | | 5 | .002 |
| O | .008 | | 4 | .133 | | 5 | .032 | | 6 | .007 |
| 1 | .062 | | | | | 6 | .084 | | 7 | .022 |
| 2 | .227 | | N = | 14 | | 7 | .180 | | 8 | .054 |
| | | | 1 | .001 | | | | | 9 | .115 |
| N = | 8 | | 2 | .006 | | N = | 20 | | 10 | .212 |
| O | .004 | | 3 | .029 | | 3 | .001 | | | |
| 1 | .035 | | 4 | .090 | | 4 | .006 | | | |
| 2 | .145 | | 5 | .212 | | 5 | .021 | | | |
| | | | | | | 6 | .058 | | | |
| N = | 9 | | N = | 15 | | 7 | .132 | | | |
| O | .002 | | 1 | .000 | | | | | | |
| 1 | .090 | | 2 | .004 | | N = | 21 | | | |
| 2 | .090 | | 3 | .018 | | 4 | .004 | | | |
| 3 | .254 | | 4 | .059 | | 5 | .013 | | | |
| | | | 5 | .151 | | 6 | .039 | | | |
| N = | 10 | | | | | 7 | .095 | | | |
| O | .001 | | N = | 16 | | 8 | .192 | | | |
| 1 | .011 | | 2 | .002 | | | | | | |
| 2 | .055 | | 3 | .011 | | N = | 22 | | | |
| 3 | .172 | | 4 | .038 | | 4 | .002 | | | |
| | | | 5 | .105 | | 5 | .008 | | | |
| | | | 6 | .227 | | 6 | .026 | | | |
| | | | | | | 7 | .067 | | | |
| | | | | | | 8 | .143 | | | |

# TABLE 5

## DISTRIBUTION FOR WILCOXON'S SIGNED-RANKS TEST

To use this table, first locate the number of **pairs** of scores in the N column. The critical values for the several levels of significance are listed in the columns to the right. For example, if N is 12 and the computed value is 9, it can be concluded that since 9 is **less** than 10, this value is significant beyond the .01 level of significance for a one-tailed test.

| N | Level of significance for one-tailed test | | |
| | .025 | .01 | .005 |
| | Level of significance for two-tailed test | | |
| | .05 | .02 | .01 |
|---|---|---|---|
| 6 | 0 | — | — |
| 7 | 2 | 0 | — |
| 8 | 4 | 2 | 0 |
| 9 | 6 | 3 | 2 |
| 10 | 8 | 5 | 3 |
| 11 | 11 | 7 | 5 |
| 12 | 14 | 10 | 7 |
| 13 | 17 | 13 | 10 |
| 14 | 21 | 16 | 13 |
| 15 | 25 | 20 | 16 |
| 16 | 30 | 24 | 19 |
| 17 | 35 | 28 | 23 |
| 18 | 40 | 33 | 28 |
| 19 | 46 | 38 | 32 |
| 20 | 52 | 43 | 37 |
| 21 | 59 | 49 | 43 |
| 22 | 66 | 56 | 49 |
| 23 | 73 | 62 | 55 |
| 24 | 81 | 69 | 61 |
| 25 | 90 | 77 | 68 |

SOURCE: Adapted from Table I of F. Wilcoxon, *Some Rapid Approximate Statistical Procedures,* rev. ed. New York: American Cyanamid Company, 1964. Reproduced from S. Siegel, *Nonparametric Statistics for the Behavioral Sciences.* New York: McGraw-Hill Book Company, 1956. Reprinted by permission of the American Cyanamid Co. and McGraw-Hill Book Co.

## TABLE 6
## SQUARES AND SQUARE ROOTS
## NOTES ON THE USE OF THE TABLE

In this table you can look up the squares and square roots of a considerable number of numbers (speaking numerically, of course). Some explanation of how to use this table might, however, be helpful:

### Squares

To find the square of any number from 1.0 to 9.99, merely look up the number under "N" in the extreme left-hand column, and under the appropriate decimal running across the top of the table. Thus, for example, to find the square of 3.75, merely find 3.7 in the first column, and then move along that row until you are under .05, and your answer is 14.06. Similarly, to find the square of 9.38, look up 9.3 in the first column, then look along that row until you are under .08, and your answer is 87.98.

For numbers over 9.99 and under 1.0, continue to use the same table, but adjust the decimal point. Thus, to find the square of 37.5, do exactly as you did for 3.75, but your answer is 1,406. To take this one step further, the square of 375 is 140,600. Going the other way, the square of .375 comes out to be .1406, and the square of .0375 is .001406. Of course, in such a relatively limited table, we do lose some precision. You cannot, for example, look up the square of 37.52 exactly, but can only get an approximation of it by looking up 37.5.

### Square Roots

As you may have noticed, the table is divided into two parts by a line along the N = 3.1 and 3.0 rows. There also is some weird gibberish in the left-hand margin, which we will now try to explain. First, it must be noted that square roots are looked up not along the margins of the table, but in the very body of it. Secondly, the line along the N = 3.1 row divides the table in such a way that the square roots of numbers extending to units (7.15, 8.4, 9.0, etc.) and numbers extending to hundreds (357.8, 293.6, 870.0) are looked up *above* that line. For example, to find the square root of 7.15, look in the *body* of the table, and you will find 7.129, followed by 7.182 along the row N = 2.6. Since 7.129 is closer to 7.15 than 7.182 is, we will use 7.129 for our approximation of the square root of 7.15. We have already determined that 7.129 is in the row N = 2.6, and if we now raise our eyes, we see that it is in the .07 column, and we can, therefore, conclude that the square root of 7.15 is approximately 2.67.

For roots of numbers extending to hundreds, we do the same thing, but we have to remember to play games with the decimal point. Thus, for example, to find the square root of 357.8, we again look for these four digits in the body of the upper part of the table, and find that the closest we can come to that is 3.572 (ignore the decimal point), which corresponds to 1.89 (n = 1.8, column headed .09); and that really is the square root of 3.572. But since we want the square root of 357.8, we have to move the decimal point in our answer one place to the right, which then makes it 18.9; and that's as close as we can get to the precise answer. You might remember that for every 2 decimal places in our original number, we have 1 decimal place in its root.

For the square roots of numbers extending to tens and thousands, you must look up the number *below* that magic line along the N = 3.1 row. For example, to find $\sqrt{21.45}$ we look for that number in the lower part of the table. The closest we can get to it is 21.44, which corresponds to 4.63, which is, indeed, $\sqrt{21.45}$. Similarly, if we want $\sqrt{89.60}$, we look for that number in the lower part of the table. What we find is 89.49 and 89.68. Our number is closer to the latter, so we will use 89.68 for our approximation, which then gives us the answer of 9.47 for the square root of 89.60.

This bottom part of the table is also to be used for looking up the square roots of numbers in the thousands, but here again we shall have to play games with the decimal points. For example, to find $\sqrt{3,555}$ we would look for those four digits in the lower part of the table, ignoring the decimal points. The closest we can get to it is 35.52, which gives us an answer of 5.96. But since we are dealing with thousands, we shall have to move the decimal point over one place, so that our final answer is 59.6.

Just to re-cap:

1. For numbers extending to units and to hundreds, use the *upper* part of the table; for numbers extending to tens and thousands, use the *lower* part of the table.

2. Most of the time, you will end up with approximations of the square root of a number. Don't worry; these approximations are close enough for anything you may wish to do without a computer.

3. This table can only handle a maximum of four digits. This means that if you want to look up $\sqrt{264.5839}$, you will first have to round it off to 264.6. This does increase the amount of error again, but only very slightly (in this case, for example, $\sqrt{264.5839}$ is really 16.266, whereas the table gives us an answer of 16.3).

4. Throughout, you can't really go wrong with the moving of decimal points, as long as you just use some common sense and see that your answer makes sense (common, that is). Thus, $\sqrt{906}$ obviously cannot be 3.01, or 9.52, or 95.2; on the other hand, 30.1 makes eminent sense. It might also help if, before diving into the table, you made an estimate of the square root you're trying to find. If, for example, you are trying to find $\sqrt{42.9}$, you should say to yourself that the answer must be somewhere between 6 (6 squared = 36) and 7 (7 squared = 49). If you then look it up and find the answer to be 6.55, you know you're OK. If you had looked it up in the wrong part of the table and had come up with an answer of 2.07 or 20.7, you would have known right away that you were in the wrong ballpark.

# TABLE 6

## SQUARES AND SQUARE ROOTS

Caution:   Read "Notes" before attempting to use!

| N | .00 | .01 | .02 | .03 | .04 | .05 | .06 | .07 | .08 | .09 |
|---|-----|-----|-----|-----|-----|-----|-----|-----|-----|-----|
| 1.0 | 1.000 | 1.020 | 1.040 | 1.061 | 1.082 | 1.103 | 1.124 | 1.145 | 1.166 | 1.188 |
| 1.1 | 1.210 | 1.232 | 1.254 | 1.277 | 1.300 | 1.323 | 1.346 | 1.369 | 1.392 | 1.416 |
| 1.2 | 1.440 | 1.464 | 1.488 | 1.513 | 1.538 | 1.563 | 1.588 | 1.613 | 1.638 | 1.664 |
| 1.3 | 1.690 | 1.716 | 1.742 | 1.769 | 1.796 | 1.823 | 1.850 | 1.877 | 1.904 | 1.932 |
| 1.4 | 1.960 | 1.988 | 2.016 | 2.045 | 2.074 | 2.103 | 2.132 | 2.161 | 2.190 | 2.220 |
| 1.5 | 2.250 | 2.280 | 2.310 | 2.341 | 2.372 | 2.403 | 2.434 | 2.465 | 2.496 | 2.528 |
| 1.6 | 2.560 | 2.592 | 2.624 | 2.657 | 2.690 | 2.723 | 2.756 | 2.789 | 2.822 | 2.856 |
| 1.7 | 2.890 | 2.924 | 2.958 | 2.993 | 3.028 | 3.063 | 3.098 | 3.133 | 3.168 | 3.204 |
| 1.8 | 3.240 | 3.276 | 3.312 | 3.349 | 3.386 | 3.423 | 3.460 | 3.497 | 3.534 | 3.572 |
| 1.9 | 3.610 | 3.648 | 3.686 | 3.725 | 3.764 | 3.803 | 3.842 | 3.881 | 3.920 | 3.960 |
| 2.0 | 4.000 | 4.040 | 4.080 | 4.121 | 4.162 | 4.203 | 4.244 | 4.285 | 4.326 | 4.368 |
| 2.1 | 4.410 | 4.452 | 4.494 | 4.537 | 4.580 | 4.623 | 4.666 | 4.709 | 4.752 | 4.796 |
| 2.2 | 4.840 | 4.884 | 4.928 | 4.973 | 5.018 | 5.063 | 5.108 | 5.153 | 5.198 | 5.244 |
| 2.3 | 5.290 | 5.336 | 5.382 | 5.429 | 5.476 | 5.523 | 5.570 | 5.617 | 5.664 | 5.712 |
| 2.4 | 5.760 | 5.808 | 5.856 | 5.905 | 5.954 | 6.003 | 6.052 | 6.101 | 6.150 | 6.200 |
| 2.5 | 6.250 | 6.300 | 6.350 | 6.401 | 6.452 | 6.503 | 6.554 | 6.605 | 6.656 | 6.708 |
| 2.6 | 6.760 | 6.812 | 6.864 | 6.917 | 6.970 | 7.023 | 7.076 | 7.129 | 7.182 | 7.236 |
| 2.7 | 7.290 | 7.344 | 7.398 | 7.453 | 7.508 | 7.563 | 7.618 | 7.673 | 7.728 | 7.784 |
| 2.8 | 7.840 | 7.896 | 7.952 | 8.009 | 8.066 | 8.123 | 8.180 | 8.237 | 8.294 | 8.352 |
| 2.9 | 8.410 | 8.468 | 8.526 | 8.585 | 8.644 | 8.703 | 8.762 | 8.821 | 8.880 | 8.940 |
| 3.0 | 9.000 | 9.060 | 9.120 | 9.181 | 9.242 | 9.303 | 9.364 | 9.425 | 9.486 | 9.548 |
| 3.1 | 9.610 | 9.672 | 9.734 | 9.797 | 9.860 | 9.923 | 9.986 | 10.05 | 10.11 | 10.18 |
| 3.2 | 10.24 | 10.30 | 10.37 | 10.43 | 10.50 | 10.56 | 10.63 | 10.69 | 10.76 | 10.82 |
| 3.3 | 10.89 | 10.96 | 11.02 | 11.09 | 11.16 | 11.22 | 11.29 | 11.36 | 11.42 | 11.49 |
| 3.4 | 11.56 | 11.63 | 11.70 | 11.76 | 11.83 | 11.90 | 11.97 | 12.04 | 12.11 | 12.18 |
| 3.5 | 12.25 | 12.32 | 12.39 | 12.46 | 12.53 | 12.60 | 12.67 | 12.74 | 12.82 | 12.89 |
| 3.6 | 12.96 | 13.03 | 13.10 | 13.18 | 13.25 | 13.32 | 13.40 | 13.47 | 13.54 | 13.62 |
| 3.7 | 13.69 | 13.76 | 13.84 | 13.91 | 13.99 | 14.06 | 14.14 | 14.21 | 14.29 | 14.36 |
| 3.8 | 14.44 | 14.52 | 14.59 | 14.67 | 14.75 | 14.82 | 14.90 | 14.98 | 15.05 | 15.13 |
| 3.9 | 15.21 | 15.29 | 15.37 | 15.44 | 15.52 | 15.60 | 15.68 | 15.76 | 15.84 | 15.92 |

**For roots of numbers extending to units (3, 3.3, 3.78, etc.) and hundreds (700, 756.8, etc.); also $\sqrt{.01-.0999}$**

**For roots of numbers extending to tens (47.5, 56.98, etc.) and thousands (3,282 or 9,123, etc.); also $\sqrt{.10-.999}$ and $\sqrt{.001-.0099}$**

*(continued on next page)*

155

TABLE 6 - Continued

## SQUARES AND SQUARE ROOTS

For roots of
numbers extending
to tens (47.5,
56.98, etc.)
and thousands
(3,282 or 9,123,
etc.); also
$\sqrt{.10-.999}$
and $\sqrt{.001-.0099}$

| N | .00 | .01 | .02 | .03 | .04 | .05 | .06 | .07 | .08 | .09 |
|-----|-------|-------|-------|-------|-------|-------|-------|-------|-------|-------|
| 4.0 | 16.00 | 16.08 | 16.16 | 16.24 | 16.32 | 16.40 | 16.48 | 16.56 | 16.65 | 16.73 |
| 4.1 | 16.81 | 16.89 | 16.97 | 17.06 | 17.14 | 17.22 | 17.31 | 17.39 | 17.47 | 17.56 |
| 4.2 | 17.64 | 17.72 | 17.81 | 17.89 | 17.98 | 18.06 | 18.15 | 18.23 | 18.32 | 18.40 |
| 4.3 | 18.49 | 18.58 | 18.66 | 18.75 | 18.84 | 18.92 | 19.01 | 19.10 | 19.18 | 19.27 |
| 4.4 | 19.36 | 19.45 | 19.54 | 19.62 | 19.71 | 19.80 | 19.89 | 19.98 | 20.07 | 20.16 |
| 4.5 | 20.25 | 20.34 | 20.43 | 20.52 | 20.61 | 20.70 | 20.79 | 20.88 | 20.98 | 21.07 |
| 4.6 | 21.16 | 21.25 | 21.34 | 21.44 | 21.53 | 21.62 | 21.72 | 21.81 | 21.90 | 22.00 |
| 4.7 | 22.09 | 22.18 | 22.28 | 22.37 | 22.47 | 22.56 | 22.66 | 22.75 | 22.85 | 22.94 |
| 4.8 | 23.04 | 23.14 | 23.23 | 23.33 | 23.43 | 23.52 | 23.62 | 23.72 | 23.81 | 23.91 |
| 4.9 | 24.01 | 24.11 | 24.21 | 24.30 | 24.40 | 24.50 | 24.60 | 24.70 | 24.80 | 24.90 |
| 5.0 | 25.00 | 25.10 | 25.20 | 25.30 | 25.40 | 25.50 | 25.60 | 25.70 | 25.81 | 25.91 |
| 5.1 | 26.01 | 26.11 | 26.21 | 26.32 | 26.42 | 26.52 | 26.63 | 26.73 | 26.83 | 26.94 |
| 5.2 | 27.04 | 27.14 | 27.25 | 27.35 | 27.46 | 27.56 | 27.67 | 27.77 | 27.88 | 27.98 |
| 5.3 | 28.09 | 28.20 | 28.30 | 28.41 | 28.52 | 28.62 | 28.73 | 28.84 | 28.94 | 29.05 |
| 5.4 | 29.16 | 29.27 | 29.38 | 29.48 | 29.59 | 29.70 | 29.81 | 29.92 | 30.03 | 30.14 |
| 5.5 | 30.25 | 30.36 | 30.47 | 30.58 | 30.69 | 30.80 | 30.91 | 31.02 | 31.14 | 31.25 |
| 5.6 | 31.36 | 31.47 | 31.58 | 31.70 | 31.81 | 31.92 | 32.04 | 32.15 | 32.26 | 32.38 |
| 5.7 | 32.49 | 32.60 | 32.72 | 32.83 | 32.95 | 33.06 | 33.18 | 33.29 | 33.41 | 33.52 |
| 5.8 | 33.64 | 33.76 | 33.87 | 33.99 | 34.11 | 34.22 | 34.34 | 34.46 | 34.57 | 34.69 |
| 5.9 | 34.81 | 34.93 | 35.05 | 35.16 | 35.28 | 35.40 | 35.52 | 35.64 | 35.76 | 35.88 |
| 6.0 | 36.00 | 36.12 | 36.24 | 36.36 | 36.48 | 36.60 | 36.72 | 36.84 | 36.97 | 37.09 |
| 6.1 | 37.21 | 37.33 | 37.45 | 37.58 | 37.70 | 37.82 | 37.95 | 38.07 | 38.19 | 38.32 |
| 6.2 | 38.44 | 38.56 | 38.69 | 38.81 | 38.94 | 39.06 | 39.19 | 39.31 | 39.44 | 39.56 |
| 6.3 | 39.69 | 39.82 | 39.94 | 40.07 | 40.20 | 40.32 | 40.45 | 40.58 | 40.70 | 40.83 |
| 6.4 | 40.96 | 41.09 | 41.22 | 41.34 | 41.47 | 41.60 | 41.73 | 41.86 | 41.99 | 42.12 |
| 6.5 | 42.25 | 42.38 | 42.51 | 42.64 | 42.77 | 42.90 | 43.03 | 43.16 | 43.30 | 43.43 |
| 6.6 | 43.56 | 43.69 | 43.82 | 43.96 | 44.09 | 44.22 | 44.36 | 44.49 | 44.62 | 44.76 |
| 6.7 | 44.89 | 45.02 | 45.16 | 45.29 | 45.43 | 45.56 | 45.70 | 45.83 | 45.97 | 46.10 |
| 6.8 | 46.24 | 46.38 | 46.51 | 46.65 | 46.79 | 46.92 | 47.06 | 47.20 | 47.33 | 47.47 |
| 6.9 | 47.61 | 47.75 | 47.89 | 48.02 | 48.16 | 48.30 | 48.44 | 48.58 | 48.72 | 48.86 |

*(continued on next page)*

TABLE 6 - Continued

## SQUARES AND SQUARE ROOTS

For roots of
numbers extending
to tens (47.5,
56.98, etc.)
and thousands
(3,282 or 9,123,
etc.); also
$\sqrt{.10-.999}$
and $\sqrt{.001-.0099}$

| N | .00 | .01 | .02 | .03 | .04 | .05 | .06 | .07 | .08 | .09 |
|---|---|---|---|---|---|---|---|---|---|---|
| 7.0 | 49.00 | 49.14 | 49.28 | 49.42 | 49.56 | 49.70 | 49.84 | 49.98 | 50.13 | 50.27 |
| 7.1 | 50.41 | 50.55 | 50.69 | 50.84 | 50.98 | 51.12 | 51.27 | 51.41 | 51.55 | 51.70 |
| 7.2 | 51.84 | 51.98 | 52.13 | 52.27 | 52.42 | 52.56 | 52.71 | 52.85 | 53.00 | 53.14 |
| 7.3 | 53.29 | 53.44 | 53.58 | 53.73 | 53.88 | 54.02 | 54.17 | 54.32 | 54.46 | 54.61 |
| 7.4 | 54.76 | 54.91 | 55.06 | 55.20 | 55.35 | 55.50 | 55.65 | 55.80 | 55.95 | 56.10 |
| 7.5 | 56.25 | 56.40 | 56.55 | 56.70 | 56.85 | 57.00 | 57.15 | 57.30 | 57.46 | 57.61 |
| 7.6 | 57.76 | 57.91 | 58.06 | 58.22 | 58.37 | 58.52 | 58.68 | 58.83 | 58.98 | 59.14 |
| 7.7 | 59.29 | 59.44 | 59.60 | 59.75 | 59.91 | 60.06 | 60.22 | 60.37 | 60.53 | 60.68 |
| 7.8 | 60.84 | 61.00 | 61.15 | 61.31 | 61.47 | 61.62 | 61.78 | 61.94 | 62.09 | 62.25 |
| 7.9 | 62.41 | 62.57 | 62.73 | 62.88 | 63.04 | 63.20 | 63.36 | 63.52 | 63.68 | 63.84 |
| 8.0 | 64.00 | 64.16 | 64.32 | 64.48 | 64.64 | 64.80 | 64.96 | 65.12 | 65.29 | 65.45 |
| 8.1 | 65.61 | 65.77 | 65.93 | 66.10 | 66.26 | 66.42 | 66.59 | 66.75 | 66.91 | 67.08 |
| 8.2 | 67.24 | 67.40 | 67.57 | 67.73 | 67.90 | 68.06 | 68.23 | 68.39 | 68.56 | 68.72 |
| 8.3 | 68.89 | 69.06 | 69.22 | 69.39 | 69.56 | 69.72 | 69.89 | 70.06 | 70.22 | 70.39 |
| 8.4 | 70.56 | 70.73 | 70.90 | 71.06 | 71.23 | 71.40 | 71.57 | 71.74 | 71.91 | 72.08 |
| 8.5 | 72.25 | 72.42 | 72.59 | 72.76 | 72.93 | 73.10 | 73.27 | 73.44 | 73.62 | 73.79 |
| 8.6 | 73.96 | 74.13 | 74.30 | 74.48 | 74.65 | 74.82 | 75.00 | 75.17 | 75.34 | 75.52 |
| 8.7 | 75.69 | 75.86 | 76.04 | 76.21 | 76.39 | 76.56 | 76.74 | 76.91 | 77.09 | 77.26 |
| 8.8 | 77.44 | 77.62 | 77.79 | 77.97 | 78.15 | 78.32 | 78.50 | 78.68 | 78.85 | 79.03 |
| 8.9 | 79.21 | 79.39 | 79.57 | 79.74 | 79.92 | 80.10 | 80.28 | 80.46 | 80.64 | 80.82 |
| 9.0 | 81.00 | 81.18 | 81.36 | 81.54 | 81.72 | 81.90 | 82.08 | 82.26 | 82.45 | 82.63 |
| 9.1 | 82.81 | 82.99 | 83.17 | 83.36 | 83.54 | 83.72 | 83.91 | 84.09 | 84.27 | 84.46 |
| 9.2 | 84.64 | 84.82 | 85.01 | 85.19 | 85,38 | 85.56 | 85.75 | 85.93 | 86.12 | 86.30 |
| 9.3 | 86.49 | 86.68 | 86.86 | 87.05 | 87.24 | 87.42 | 87.61 | 87.80 | 87.98 | 88.17 |
| 9.4 | 88.36 | 88.55 | 88.74 | 88.92 | 89.11 | 89.30 | 89.49 | 89.68 | 89.87 | 90.06 |
| 9.5 | 90.25 | 90.44 | 90.63 | 90.82 | 91.01 | 91.20 | 91.39 | 91.58 | 91.78 | 91.97 |
| 9.6 | 92.16 | 92.35 | 92.54 | 92.74 | 92.93 | 93.12 | 93.32 | 93.51 | 93.70 | 93.90 |
| 9.7 | 94.09 | 94.28 | 94.48 | 94.67 | 94.87 | 95.06 | 95.26 | 95.45 | 95.65 | 95.84 |
| 9.8 | 96.04 | 96.24 | 96.43 | 96.63 | 96.83 | 97.02 | 97.22 | 97.42 | 97.61 | 97.81 |
| 9.9 | 98.01 | 98.21 | 98.41 | 98.60 | 98.80 | 99.00 | 99.20 | 99.40 | 99.60 | 99.80 |

# TABLE 7

## RANDOM NUMBERS*

```
10 09 73 25 33    76 52 01 35 86    34 67 35 48 76    80 95 90 91 17    39 29 27 49 45
37 54 20 48 05    64 89 47 42 96    24 80 52 40 37    20 63 61 04 02    00 82 29 16 65
08 42 26 89 53    19 64 50 93 03    23 20 90 25 60    15 95 33 47 64    35 08 03 36 06
99 01 90 25 29    09 37 67 07 15    38 31 13 11 65    88 67 67 43 97    04 43 62 76 59
12 80 79 99 70    80 15 73 61 47    64 03 23 66 53    98 95 11 68 77    12 17 17 68 33

66 06 57 47 17    34 07 27 68 50    36 69 73 61 70    65 81 33 98 85    11 19 92 91 70
31 06 01 08 05    45 57 18 24 06    35 30 34 26 14    86 79 90 74 39    23 40 30 97 32
85 26 97 76 02    02 05 16 56 92    68 66 57 48 18    73 05 38 52 47    18 62 38 85 79
63 57 33 21 35    05 32 54 70 48    90 55 35 75 48    28 46 82 87 09    83 49 12 56 24
73 79 64 57 53    03 52 96 47 78    35 80 83 42 82    60 93 52 03 44    35 27 38 84 35

98 52 01 77 67    14 90 56 86 07    22 10 94 95 58    60 97 09 34 33    50 50 07 39 98
11 80 50 54 31    39 80 82 77 32    50 72 56 82 48    29 40 52 42 01    52 77 56 78 51
83 45 29 96 34    06 28 89 80 83    13 74 67 00 78    18 47 54 06 10    68 71 17 78 17
88 68 54 02 00    86 50 75 84 01    36 76 66 79 51    90 36 47 64 93    29 60 91 10 62
99 59 46 73 48    87 51 76 49 69    91 82 60 89 28    93 78 56 13 68    23 47 83 41 13

65 48 11 76 74    17 46 85 09 50    58 04 77 69 74    73 03 95 71 86    40 21 81 65 44
80 12 43 56 35    17 72 70 80 15    45 31 82 23 74    21 11 57 82 53    14 38 55 37 63
74 35 09 98 17    77 40 27 72 14    43 23 60 02 10    45 52 16 42 37    96 28 60 26 55
69 91 62 68 03    66 25 22 91 48    36 93 68 72 03    76 62 11 39 90    94 40 05 64 18
09 89 32 05 05    14 22 56 85 14    46 42 75 67 88    96 29 77 88 22    54 38 21 45 98

91 49 91 45 23    68 47 92 76 86    46 16 28 35 54    94 75 08 99 23    37 08 92 00 48
80 33 69 45 98    26 94 03 68 58    70 29 73 41 35    53 14 03 33 40    42 05 08 23 41
44 10 48 19 49    85 15 74 79 54    32 97 92 65 75    57 60 04 08 81    22 22 20 64 13
12 55 07 37 42    11 10 00 20 40    12 86 07 46 97    96 64 48 94 39    28 70 72 58 15
63 60 64 93 29    16 50 53 44 84    40 21 95 25 63    43 65 17 70 82    07 20 73 17 90

61 19 69 04 46    26 45 74 77 74    51 92 43 37 29    65 39 45 95 93    42 58 26 05 27
15 47 44 52 66    95 27 07 99 53    59 36 78 38 48    82 39 61 01 18    33 21 15 94 66
94 55 72 85 73    67 89 75 43 87    54 62 24 44 31    91 19 04 25 92    92 92 74 59 73
42 48 11 62 13    97 34 40 87 21    16 86 84 87 67    03 07 11 20 59    25 70 14 66 70
23 52 37 83 17    73 20 88 98 37    68 93 59 14 16    26 25 22 96 63    05 52 28 25 62

04 49 35 24 94    75 24 63 38 24    45 86 25 10 25    61 96 27 93 35    65 33 71 24 72
00 54 99 76 54    64 05 18 81 59    96 11 96 38 96    54 69 28 23 91    23 28 72 95 29
35 96 31 53 07    26 89 80 93 54    33 35 13 54 62    77 97 45 00 24    90 10 33 93 33
59 80 80 83 91    45 42 72 68 42    83 60 94 97 00    13 02 12 48 92    78 56 52 01 06
46 05 88 52 36    01 39 09 22 86    77 28 14 40 77    93 91 08 36 47    70 61 74 29 41
```

*(continued on next page)*

*This table is reproduced with permission from tables of the RAND Corporation.

TABLE 7 - Continued

## RANDOM NUMBERS

```
32 17 90 05 97    87 37 92 52 41    05 56 70 70 07    86 74 31 71 57    85 39 41 18 38
69 23 46 14 06    20 11 74 52 04    15 95 66 00 00    18 74 39 24 23    97 11 89 63 38
19 56 54 14 30    01 75 87 53 79    40 41 92 15 85    66 67 43 68 06    84 96 28 52 07
45 15 51 49 38    19 47 60 72 46    43 66 79 45 43    59 04 79 00 33    20 82 66 95 41
94 86 43 19 94    36 16 81 08 51    34 88 88 15 53    01 54 03 54 56    05 01 45 11 76

98 08 62 48 26    45 24 02 84 04    44 99 90 88 96    39 09 47 34 07    35 44 13 18 80
33 18 51 62 32    41 94 15 09 49    89 43 54 85 81    88 69 54 19 94    37 54 87 30 43
80 95 10 04 06    96 38 27 07 74    20 15 12 33 87    25 01 62 52 98    94 62 46 11 71
79 75 24 91 40    71 96 12 82 96    69 86 10 25 91    74 85 22 05 39    00 38 75 95 79
18 63 33 25 37    98 14 50 65 71    31 01 02 46 74    05 45 56 14 27    77 93 89 19 36

74 02 94 39 02    77 55 73 22 70    97 79 01 71 19    52 52 75 80 21    80 81 45 17 48
54 17 84 56 11    80 99 33 71 43    05 33 51 29 69    56 12 71 92 55    36 04 09 03 24
11 66 44 98 83    52 07 98 48 27    59 38 17 15 39    09 97 33 34 40    88 46 12 33 56
48 32 47 79 28    31 24 96 47 10    02 29 53 68 70    32 30 75 75 46    15 02 00 99 94
69 07 49 41 38    87 63 79 19 76    35 58 40 44 01    10 51 82 16 15    01 84 87 69 38

09 18 82 00 97    32 82 53 95 27    04 22 08 63 04    83 38 98 73 74    64 27 85 80 44
90 04 58 54 97    51 98 15 06 54    94 93 88 19 97    91 87 07 61 50    68 47 66 46 59
73 18 95 02 07    47 67 72 62 69    62 29 06 44 64    27 12 46 70 18    41 36 18 27 60
75 76 87 64 90    20 97 18 17 49    90 42 91 22 72    95 37 50 58 71    93 82 34 31 78
54 01 64 40 56    66 28 13 10 03    00 68 22 73 98    20 71 45 32 95    07 70 61 78 13

08 35 86 99 10    78 54 24 27 85    13 66 15 88 73    04 61 89 75 53    31 22 30 84 20
28 30 60 32 64    81 33 31 05 91    40 51 00 78 93    32 60 46 04 75    94 11 90 18 40
53 84 08 62 33    81 59 41 36 28    51 21 59 02 90    28 46 66 87 95    77 76 22 07 91
91 75 75 37 41    61 61 36 22 69    50 26 39 01 12    55 78 17 65 14    83 48 34 70 55
89 41 59 26 94    00 39 75 83 91    12 60 71 76 46    48 94 97 23 06    94 54 13 74 08

77 51 30 38 20    86 83 42 99 01    68 41 48 27 74    51 90 81 39 80    72 89 35 55 07
19 50 23 71 74    69 97 92 02 88    55 21 02 97 73    74 28 77 52 51    65 34 46 74 15
21 81 85 93 13    93 27 88 17 57    05 68 67 31 56    07 08 28 50 46    31 85 33 84 52
51 47 46 64 99    68 10 72 36 21    94 04 99 13 45    42 83 60 91 91    08 00 74 54 49
99 55 96 83 31    62 53 52 41 70    69 77 71 28 30    74 81 97 81 42    43 86 07 28 34

33 71 34 80 07    93 58 47 28 69    51 92 66 47 21    58 30 32 98 22    93 17 49 39 72
85 27 48 68 93    11 30 32 92 70    28 83 43 41 37    73 51 59 04 00    71 14 84 36 43
84 13 38 96 40    44 03 55 21 66    73 85 27 00 91    61 22 26 05 61    62 32 71 84 23
56 73 21 62 34    17 39 59 61 31    10 12 39 16 22    85 49 65 75 60    81 60 41 88 80
65 13 85 68 06    87 64 88 52 61    34 31 36 58 61    45 87 52 10 69    85 64 44 72 77
```

*(continued on next page)*

TABLE 7 - Continued

## RANDOM NUMBERS

```
38 00 10 21 76    81 71 91 17 11    71 60 29 29 37    74 21 96 40 49    65 58 44 96 98
37 40 29 63 97    01 30 47 75 86    56 27 11 00 86    47 32 46 26 05    40 03 03 74 38
97 12 54 03 48    87 08 33 14 17    21 81 53 92 50    75 23 76 20 47    15 50 12 95 78
21 82 64 11 34    47 14 33 40 72    64 63 88 59 02    49 13 90 64 41    03 85 65 45 52
73 13 54 27 42    95 71 90 90 35    85 79 47 42 96    08 78 98 81 56    64 69 11 92 02

07 63 87 79 29    03 06 11 80 72    96 20 74 41 56    23 82 19 95 38    04 71 36 69 94
60 52 88 34 41    07 95 41 98 14    59 17 52 06 95    05 53 35 21 39    61 21 20 64 55
83 59 63 56 55    06 95 89 29 83    05 12 80 97 19    77 43 35 37 83    92 30 15 04 98
10 85 06 27 46    99 59 91 05 07    13 49 90 63 19    53 07 57 18 39    06 41 01 93 62
39 82 09 89 52    43 62 26 31 47    64 42 18 08 14    43 80 00 93 51    31 02 47 31 67

59 58 00 64 78    75 56 97 88 00    88 83 55 44 86    23 76 80 61 56    04 11 10 84 08
38 50 80 73 41    23 79 34 87 63    90 82 29 70 22    17 71 90 42 07    95 95 44 99 53
30 69 27 06 68    94 68 81 61 27    56 19 68 00 91    82 06 76 34 00    05 46 26 92 00
65 44 39 56 59    18 28 82 74 37    49 63 22 40 41    08 33 76 56 76    96 29 99 08 36
27 26 75 02 64    13 19 27 22 94    07 47 74 46 06    17 98 54 89 11    97 34 13 03 58

91 30 70 69 91    10 07 22 42 10    36 69 95 37 28    28 82 53 57 93    28 97 66 62 52
68 43 49 46 88    84 47 31 36 22    62 12 69 84 08    12 84 38 25 90    09 81 59 31 46
48 90 81 58 77    54 74 52 45 91    35 70 00 47 54    83 82 45 26 92    54 13 05 51 60
06 91 34 51 97    42 67 27 86 01    11 88 30 95 28    63 01 19 89 01    14 97 44 03 44
10 45 51 60 19    14 21 03 37 12    91 34 23 78 21    88 32 58 08 51    43 66 77 08 83

12 88 39 73 43    65 02 76 11 84    04 28 50 13 92    17 97 41 50 77    90 71 22 67 69
21 77 83 09 76    38 80 73 69 61    31 64 94 20 96    63 28 10 20 23    08 81 64 74 49
19 52 35 95 15    65 12 25 96 59    86 28 36 82 58    69 57 21 37 98    16 43 59 15 29
67 24 55 26 70    35 58 31 65 63    79 24 68 66 86    76 46 33 42 22    26 65 59 08 02
60 58 44 73 77    07 50 03 79 92    45 13 42 65 29    26 76 08 36 37    41 32 64 43 44

58 85 34 13 77    36 06 69 48 50    58 83 87 38 59    49 36 47 33 31    96 24 04 36 42
24 63 73 87 36    74 38 48 93 42    52 62 30 79 92    12 36 91 86 01    03 74 28 38 73
83 08 01 24 51    38 99 22 28 15    07 75 95 17 77    97 37 72 75 85    51 97 23 78 67
16 44 42 43 34    36 15 19 90 73    27 49 37 09 39    85 13 03 25 52    54 84 65 47 59
60 79 01 81 57    57 17 86 57 62    11 16 17 85 76    45 81 95 29 79    65 13 00 48 60
```

**APPENDIX B**

**ANSWERS TO SELECTED PROBLEMS**

**Chapter 2**

1. a) $\dfrac{23}{30}$     c) $2\dfrac{1}{4}$     e) $6\dfrac{47}{72}$

2. a) $\dfrac{1}{8}$     c) $\dfrac{20}{21}$

3. a) $\dfrac{1}{20}$     c) $5\dfrac{1}{24}$

4. a) $\dfrac{6}{7}$     c) $\dfrac{15}{23}$

5. a) .7059; 70.59%     c) $\dfrac{9}{25}$ ; .36

    e) $\dfrac{79}{100}$ ; 79%     g) .875; 87.5%

    i) $\dfrac{913}{2500}$ ; .3652     k) $3\dfrac{22}{125}$ ; 317.6%

    m) 4.6667; 466.67%     o) $\dfrac{2}{625}$ ; .0032

6. a) 3.842     c) 6,917     e) 9.61

    g) $\sim$ 2304 ( $\sim$ means approximately)     i) $\sim$ 6.1

    k) 1.36     m) $\sim$ 4.07     o) $\sim$ 15.4

    q) $\sim$ 54.8     s) $\sim$ 90.8

7. a) 57     c) 630     e) 1.25

    g) 188.887

8. b) 1.244

**Chapter 4**

1. a) 77.78%     c) 25.86%

    e) USD; ratio of single females to single males here is 6:5, which is better than 8:7 or 7:10.

2. 

| Score | F | CF | % | Percentile |
|-------|---|-----|----|-----------|
| 96 | 1 | 25 | 4 | 100 |
| 95 | 0 | 24 | 0 | 96 |
| 94 | 0 | 24 | 0 | 96 |
| 93 | 0 | 24 | 0 | 96 |
| 92 | 1 | 24 | 4 | 96 |
| 91 | 1 | 23 | 4 | 92 |
| 90 | 1 | 22 | 4 | 88 |
| 89 | 2 | 21 | 8 | 84 |
| 88 | 3 | 19 | 12 | 76 |
| 87 | 4 | 16 | 16 | 64 |
| 86 | 5 | 12 | 20 | 48 |
| 85 | 4 | 7 | 16 | 28 |
| 84 | 3 | 3 | 12 | 12 |
| Total | 25 | — | 100 | — |

4. a)

| Sex | F |
|-----|---|
| male | 14 |
| female | 16 |
| Total | 30 |

14:16 or 7:8

**Chapter 5**

1. a) 7.05; 6.975; 7.0

   b) 7.0 or 7.5 for all groups

   c) 7.0 for all groups

2. a) Group A – 10.834; Group C – 7.56

   b) Group A – 10.82;  Group C – 7.2

   c) Group A – 11.0;   Group C – 7.0

3. a) Mean can not be calculated for Total and Family cases (note "300 and over" interval). For One-Person cases mean = $69.40

   b) Total cases – $93.31; One-person – $69.07; Family–?

4. a) median;          c)  mean

6. 1940 –  mean =   31.75 yrs
          median = 29.07 yrs
          mode =   15 yrs

   1976 –  mean =   33.5 yrs
          median = 29.075 yrs
          mode =   15 yrs

**Chapter 6**    1.  Group A has the greatest variability.
Group B has the least variability.
The s.d. for Group C is 1.09 yrs.

2.  Group A—Range = 10 yrs.
Group C—Range = 8 yrs.

3.  a)  50.85 yrs.

    b)  16.90 yrs.

    c)  47.875 yrs.

4.  1940 standard deviation = 20.26 yrs.
1976 standard deviation = 22.04 yrs.

**Chapter 7**    1.  a)  .159 or 15.9%      c)  .10      e)  .025

        g)  .036                i)  .308

    2.  a)  27.8%         c)  4.0%      e)  .5%

        g)  98%           i)  97.6%

    3.  a)  15.9%; 84.1%      c)  2.3%; 97.7%

        e)  ~ 86%;  ~ 24%

    4.  e)  $z = -.5$; 69.2% above;  30.8% below

        g)  $z = 2.3$; 1.1% above; 98.9% below

        i)  $z = -.9$; 81.6% above; 18.4% below

    5.  e)  127.2 lbs.      g)  ~ 146.6 lbs. and 173.4 lbs.

        i)  108 lbs and 212 lbs.

**Chapter 8**    2.  a)  2.5 yrs.      c)  .055      e)  1.67 yrs.; —; .008; —

    3.  a)  .102, or approx. .1;    c)  .159

        e)  .07; —; .08; —

4. a) .945                    b) .994

5. a) .682              c) .023              e) 154.5 lbs.

   g) $\sim$ 157.8 lbs. and 162.16 lbs.

   i) 151.42 lbs. and 168.58 lbs.


**Chapter 9**   1. Note meaning of "unsurpassed." Hypothesis might have been: Aspirin is better than Abacin. If level of significance is set at .001, for example, there will be a strong tendency to keep null hypothesis: Abacin = Aspirin; therefore, it is "unsurpassed."

2. $p < .01$

3. a) keep $H_o$              c) reject $H_o$

   e) reject $H_o$           g) reject $H_o$
   i) reject $H_o$

4. $p < .001$

5. h) $p < .01$

6. h) $p \cong .04$

7. h) $p \cong .018$


**Chapter 10**   1. h) $t = -2.79$

2. j) $t = .71$

4. f) $t = 1.81$

6. $t = .34$

7. $t = 1.71$


**Chapter 11**   1. $\chi^2 = 7.44$

2. $\chi^2 = 1.09$

3. $\chi^2 = 4.6$

4.  d) $iX^2 = 4.7$

5.  g) $p < .01$

**Chapter 12**  2.  a) $r = .687$; $t = 2.67$; $p < .025$ (directional); $r^2 = .472$

   b) $r = .313$; $t = .932$; $p > .10$; $r^2 = .098$

   c) $rho = .139$; $t = .397$; $p > .10$; $r^2 = .019$

3.  $rho = .745$

4.  $rho = .842$

5.  $rho = .813$; $t = 4.63$

6.  Instrument I. $- r = .931$
    Instrument II.$- r = .625$

| 7. | Age | Health | Financial | Life Sat. | Anomie |
|---|---|---|---|---|---|
| Age | 1.00 | $-.767$*** | $-.42$** | .336* | .003 |
| Health | | 1.00 | | | |
| Financial | | | 1.00 | | |
| Life Sat. | | | | 1.00 | |
| Anomie | | | | | 1.00 |

   ***$p < .01$
    **$p < .05$
     *$p < .10$

**Chapter 13**  1.  a) $p = .062$          b) $p = .025$

2.  a) $p = .033$          b) no need to

3.  a) $p = .023$          b) $p < .01$

4.  $\phi = .135$

5.  $C = .21$

6.  $\phi = .217$

7.  $C = .36$

# INDEX

Error
     standard, of mean, 69-75
     Type I & Type II, 87
Estimated standard error of the mean, 97-98
Estimated standard error of difference between two
  means, 100-101
Expected frequency, 113-116

Fable, 85-86
Fractions, 3-5
Freedom, degrees of, 95-96
Frequency, cumulative, 25-26
     expected, 113-116
     observed, 113-116
Frequency distribution, 23, 25, 28-29
     and arithmetic mean, 40-45
     asymmetrical, 56-57
     definition, 23
     graphical methods of describing, 49, 55-59
     and indicators of central tendency, 35-45
     normal, 58-62
     standard deviation, 49-54
     skewed, 56-57
     symmetrical, 57
     z-score, 61-62
Frequency polygons, 57-58

Guessed mean, 42-45

Histograms, 49
Hypotheses, alternate (or alternative), 84
     directional, 84, 106-109
     non-directional, 84, 106-109
     null, 84
Hypothesis Testing, 88-92 (also see Tests)

Improbable outcomes, 83-85
Intervals, class, 29-30
Interval variables, 18, 27-29

Levels of significance, 84-87

Mean, 40-45
     compared with median, mode, 45
     computation of, simple distribution, 41
     computation of, grouped data, 41-43
     estimated standard error, 98-99
     guessed, 42-45
     sampling distribution, 68-75
     standard error, 69-75
Means, differences between, 100-103

Median, 37-40
     compared with mean and mode, 45
     computation of, simple distribution, 37
     computation of, grouped data, 38-40
Midpoint of class interval, 30
     coded, 42-44
Modal interval (category), 25, 37
Mode, 25, 35-37
     compared with mean, median, 45
Multimodal distribution, 36-37
Multi-stage sampling (see Cluster sample)

Names, values stated by, 17
Nominal variables, 17, 22-25
Non-directional hypothesis, 84, 106-109
Non-parametric tests, 137
Non-probability samples, 66
     Accidental samples, 66
     Available data, 66
     convenience samples, 66
     Purposive samples, 66
     Quota samples, 66
Non-random samples (see non-probability samples)
Normal curve, 56-64
     determining probabilities by, 60-64
     significance tests and, 89-92
     and t-distribution, compared, 96-97
     table of, 148
Normal curve tests, effect of small samples
  on, 69-70, 72-75
Normal distribution, 56-64
     characteristics, 59
     of means, 68-75
     and standard score, 61-62
     and z scores, 61-62
Null hypotheses, 84
     alternate hypotheses and, 84, 106-109
     errors and, 87
     and levels of significance, 87
     rejection, 87
     risk of acceptance, 87
     testing, 88-92, 95-109
Numbers, 16-17
     negative, 9-10
     in formulas, 11

Observed frequency, 113-116
One- and two-tailed tests, 104-109
Ordinal variables, 17-18, 25-26

Percentages, 6
     use of, 23-25